# The
# Faith of
# Christ Jesus

## Lost on Planet Earth

*Understanding Why Faith is Misunderstood*

Compiled with Commentary by

# George K. Somerville, D.Phil.

Post Gutenberg™

AN IMPRINT OF
GLOBALEDADVANCEPRESS

**THE FAITH OF CHRIST JESUS**

**Lost on Planet Earth**

Copyright © 2013 by George K. Somerville

Library of Congress Control Number: 2013931925

Somerville, George K., 1934-

 The Faith of Christ Jesus: Lost on Planet Earth

 ISBN 978-1-935434-16-0

 Subject Codes and Description:

 1. REL012000: Religion: Christian Life - General  2. REL. 012040: Religion: Christian Life - Inspirational  3. REL 006080 Religion: Biblical Criticism and Interpretation-General

Cover design by Global Graphics

Printed in Australia, Brazil, France, Germany, Italy, Spain, UK, and USA.

Published by
Post-Gutenberg Books™
An Imprint of
GlobalEdAdvancePress

# Dedication

To my wife Shirley,
who as always, stands ready
to discern and to encourage.

and

Thank you Olga Smith,
in your anticipation of another book, and used of the Lord
to convict and inspire one who knows the need,
the writing of this book is dedicated.

# Acknowledgement

## Destroyed Foundations
### Charles R. Solomon, Ed.D.

1. Our country is on the ropes with foundations being destroyed - As God's presence is disunited, rendering the Constitution null and void.

2. A country of, by, and for the people is based on mutual trust: with the common good being ignored, the Church's leadership is a must!

3. Only God's sovereign intervention can change history's flow: the problem of consummate selfishness can only spiritual resolution know?

4. The Church must give the answer that involves life transformation. But it can only be dispensed as we know a completed Reformation.

5. As with a person, so with the Church, desperation is the driving force: at the limit of our extremity, Jesus Christ is our only source.

6. Obviously, the Church must be awakened to its vital role in the present situation; with lost authority being regained, only Holy God can do an intervention.

7. Man has plundered Earth's resources in a vain search for meaning: the Church, too, has joined the fray in all the wrong places gleaning.

8. Now, the Church must lead the world by returning to preaching the cross; (1 Cor. 1:18) Only as lives are so transformed will Church and world turn from loss?

9. Our God is more than able to hear our frantic cries: only losing our lives to save them (Luke 9:23,24) will conquer Satan's lies.

# Table of Contents

*"...Jesus finished the task,
assigned faith to those who believe,
and sat down at the right hand of the Father.
Jesus rested."*

# Author's Preface

Faith is an issue of our time. Since Israel became a nation, faith, for many religious movements is 'Lost on Planet Earth.' The point of concern lay in the where, when, what, how, and why is faith so misunderstood? Is it because of what Jesus said about finding faith on earth upon His return? This question, grievous to the Lord, weighs heavily upon many a heart. His return is imminent, but only God the Father knows. Nevertheless, happy are those, when He comes He shall find watching. Only through the faith of His Beloved Son, will anyone see the Glory of the Father, revealed. (Luke 12:27)

In Faith, "God created man in His own image, in the image of God created He him; male and female created He them. For by Him were all things created, that are in heaven, and that are in earth, visible and invisible, whether they be thrones, or dominions, principalities, or powers: all things were created by Him, and for Him." Science continues to make fools of the wise, in search for a missing link that will show man coming out of the water. (Col. 1:16, Gen. 1:27)

In preparation for this study, the word "faith" was searched. Google returned millions of results. By definition, Wikipedia, the free online encyclopedia, defined faith as "the confidence or trust in a person or entity; faith is belief in a single god or multiple gods in teaching religion."[1]  Evidence of faith is the selection of assumptions determined by reason, or else mere conjecture, or superstition.

This, in contrast with Biblical scholars who rest their faith on Heb. 11:1 "Now faith is the substance of things hoped for, the evidence of things not seen." Looking unto Jesus the Author and Finisher of our faith; who for the joy that was set before Him endured the cross, despising the shame, sat down at the right hand of the throne of God." This assures us that Christ, the Finisher of Faith, is our faith. (Heb. 12:2)

The latter scripture reference suggests Jesus finished the task, assigned faith to those who believe, and sat down at the right hand of the Father. Jesus rested. Faith, attached to the past with knowledge of tomorrow, we too enter that rest assured from the foundation of the world. Christ Jesus, when faced with imminent death, cried out unto the Father, "My God, My God, why have you forsaken me?" Christ, became sin, upon which, the Father could not look. We, made the righteousness of God in Christ Jesus, stand in Him giving testimony unto the world. (Mat. 27:46; 2 Cor. 5:21; Heb. 4:3)

There is no clear definition of faith. Except, we know it is a gift of God given to the faithful in Christ. Some explain faith to children by having them sit down on a chair, trusting that the one standing behind will not pull it away, causing a fall. In childlike trust, a child will usually sit down. Jesus said, "Forbid not the little children, let them come to me, because such is the kingdom of heaven." A child has yet to have trust shattered by lies and deceit, the assurance of a flower that will surely bear good fruit. At what age does a child begin to doubt? Is there an age of innocence, wherein a child loses the right to salvation? Is there an age of accountability? Are they not also born in sin? (Mat. 19:4; Luke 18:16; Eph. 1:1)

In most religious movements, there is no assurance of faith, but rather questions of doubt. Hoping truth shall set them free many prefer to rest on sight, rationalized by feelings. How many times have you sat down without first looking to make sure its safe? Christians, buy into bondage by sight, do so in knowledge of truth, blinded by emotion.

As we move into the introduction, and subsequent chapters, please have a King James Version of the Bible for reference. Although, there may be some paraphrasing, or alternate use of a modern version, the older versions may be more reliable in understanding the many aspects of faith dealt with in this book.

Natural men tend to spin for themselves a tale of opinions out of intellect, just to have a religion they may call their own. Many are eager and ready to make a personal faith made up of sight rather than to receive that which God has formed for those who trust. Most prefer natural doctrines that fancy good times and pleasure, rather than a supernatural teaching, calling one unto death, burial, and resurrection.

Many years now past since the author acknowledged his death, burial, and resurrection. The truth shall set you free. The truth, you must be crucified with Christ who said, "If any man will come after me, let him deny himself, and take up his cross daily, and follow me. (Luke 9:23; Gal. 2:20)

This book, written to men and women of faith who look for truth to set them free, may access and read in their leisure. Crucial to the twenty first century, this book does not apologize for any content of truth that may show bias in laying out the way of truth and eternal Life. However, look around and with full assurance of faith, move into areas of truth that regard the faith of the fathers. Traditions of those gone before brought the Gospel of salvation to planet earth, to the saved through the Faith of the Lord Jesus Christ.

*"Faith is not a feeling, nor does it come from works. It has intellectual worth."*

# Introduction

Does faith have purpose, or should we think of it as trust? In keeping with the Word of God, and understanding the purpose of faith, we need to know the source of faith: where does it originate? According to scripture, faith comes by hearing, hearing of the Word of God: not according to knowledge, or workings of mind. (Rom. 10:17, Gal. 3:2-5) Napoleon wrote, "All the scholastic scaffolding falls, as a ruined edifice, before one single word – faith."[37] What we need to determine is what purpose faith has in scholastic scaffolding.

According to one suggested reference, trust can be traced to a neurobiological structure of the human brain, and is but a social activity. Here then, we have need for a scholastic scaffold. One by which we reach levels of social activity not hitherto known. Society plays out its role as an interactivity of relationships between people, and display an attribute of trust as a means of avoiding misunderstanding.[1] Trust in this context, is a scholastic scaffold of faith in practice.

The contract is an example of faith as a scaffold in practice. In a hearing, trust argued in court with words of agreement, is a societal activity. One of the challenges of scholastic science is to re-think how the process of trust affects the construct of society. This is true when information is such that it alters human behavior within a social network. A contract becomes the word of the law in any social activity.

In society, trust and faith take many paths. Uncertainty for instance, leads to risk of failure or harm, particularly when one does not behave as instructed. Trust and faith, when attributed to relations between people of different religions have a problem. Many have places to go, better things to do than argue over matters of trust and faith. In practice, what level should the scaffold of faith reach? This, in part, is what the book attempts to put forth as scholastic.

In society, the degree to which one trusts in another is a measure of good will. Confidence therefore, is comparable to trust. Confidence, in the form of a belief system, measures the competence of another. Incompetence, when interpreted as failure, is the lack of trust, and good will toward another.

A treacherous pathway to trust is rationality. This model of belief exists because of threat. Rationality, when recognized as a belief system, is an attribute of the mind dealing with stress resulting from threat. Faith, on the other hand, is a belief system modeled through an attribute given of Christ. Inspiration, revealed by the reality of absolute authority, tends toward spirituality. Faith is the channel for Christian belief. Trust on the other hand, is a rationale of reason, the level of social intelligence leading to doubt and disparity.

The Bible teaches that Faith comes by hearing the word of God. (Rom. 10:17) Unfortunately, not all churches teach the Word of God as inspired. Doubt in the authority of the Word of God, is lack of faith.[2] Human learning, those with the blessings of God upon it, introduce us to divine wisdom, and while we study the works of nature, in which the God of all nature manifests Himself.

Biblical Hebrew, Greek, and Aramaic, translated into English allows for some degree of flexibility. Faith, coming through hearing the Word of God, and inspired by the power of the Holy Spirit reveals the Word of God according to promise. That measure of faith, leading to forgiveness and salvation, is a gift from God without which, there is no hope for eternal Life. Language then, is an interpreted scholastic idiom. This book takes advantage, in a limited way, to express an idea or concept as commentary, without straying far off the path.

In these few chapters, we look at how variables of faith compromise its efficacy on Christian life and teaching. We show how meaning, readily changed by the insertion or the omission of a single preposition, affects the interpretation of the Word. The great commission is about going, teaching all nations, baptizing them in the name of the Father, and of the Son, and of the Holy Ghost. The Lord has given them faith to believe, wherein the commission now is to follow through to build upon that faith.

This book introduces observed phenomenon of religion. The chapters based on Living Systems variables, form a network of communication links attributed to the Channel and Net.[29] The book Living Systems, outlines eight levels of systems and comparable behaviors. Following scholastic scaffolding, each variable identifies the behavior of the human organism. Each chapter and title reflects Meaning, Sort, Threshold, Pattern, Distortion, Ratio, Lack, and Cost of living faith in Christ.

It is more than two thousand years since the resurrection of Christ. Faith is not a feeling, nor does it come from works. It has intellectual worth. The Faith of Christ is received by the listening ear. Faith comes by hearing, and that of listening to the Word of God. Patience is a virtue of the Lord. The eternal Christ: the same yesterday, today, and forever, shall He find faith on His return to planet earth?

There is order in the plan of God's eternal salvation. True understanding of faith is personal, persistent, and experiential in hearing the Word of God. Upon hearing the Word of Truth, learn to trust the gospel of salvation. Christ is our salvation by which we believe, sealed with the Holy Spirit of promise. The Spirit is guarantor of inheritance until the redemption of our body, His purchased possession. (Eph. 1:13-14)

Over the years, secular and religious philosophers conclude that reason leads to pessimism. Liberal thinking persons do not accept the Bible as a true measure of humanity.[9] The Bible, to this age of reason, is full of mistakes, but nonetheless provides an answer to the need for a true religious experience.

This book, written for Christians, does not reveal the many affects liberalism has on theological thinkers. The author, over the past fifty years, rejected the theologian's interpretation of the Word of God as positional, progressive, and/or conditional. Being assured in the Faith of Christ, the author stands on the Word of God as absolute, changeless, and authoritative. There is no equal in life and Christian practice.

CHAPTER ONE

# Meaning:
# The Measure of Faith

The "Faith of Christ Jesus" subtitled: "Lost on planet Earth" takes its reference from the story of a widow seeking justice from one who had no fear of God or man. The story illustrates the need to walk by faith, and never give up. The widow wanted to file suit against an adversary. The judge, unwilling at first, but due to her persistence, granted her request. (Luke 18:1-8) Upon finishing the story Jesus said, "When the Son of Man comes, shall He find faith on earth?" What is the connection, if any, between the widow, the false judge, and the meaning of persistence? The quotation seems out of context. What did the Lord really mean by that remark? Is it just a casual response, or is there something significant here in context?

In pondering the quotation, would it be conceivable to think He is referring to His return for the church, the rapture, or some other future event? This book is about what man has forgotten. In the two thousand years since the ascension, many, many things happened, well beyond the scope of any reference library. It seems fitting to suggest something is missing, surreal, odd, a dreamlike quality of expression like, "He ain't comin back!" Without controversy, great is the mystery of godliness: God was revealed in flesh, justified in the Spirit, seen of angels, preached to all nations, believed on in the world, now received up into glory. How can it be that there is something missing? This book reveals some startling facts, not hitherto known to Christian. (1 Tim. 3:16)

Mathew Henry in commentary suggests that humanity, and in particular, Israel, lost faith in what the New Testament teaches about the return of Christ on planet earth. The number of references to His return are numerous. However, in all the references, it does not mention what. In His remark Jesus is saying, "I'll be back for those of faith." Suppose that when He does come back, there is little or no faith.

In general, a few good people may be found. Perhaps those who practice some form of righteousness, and honesty, but those of faith, very few. Henry suggests Christ will delay His coming so long as wicked people are in defiance. He may delay His return as this will go toward the hardening of the heart, even when the people of Israel are in despair. One thing for sure, the unbelieving race of humanity has not, and will not make the promise of His return of no effect.[32]

There is great misunderstanding over what we must believe. Pretending that doubt does not exist, and then whatever we believe will happen, absurd. Many formulate their own plans and then present them to God, muster up faith of their own by human effort and then expect God to act. Why not just wish upon a star, a four-leaf clover, or a lucky charm. The image of the cross is quite prevalent among artifacts hung about the neck, or charm bracelet upon the wrist and ankle. These are quite in vogue in this unbelieving culture. When God does not do as expected, and according to some, He should believe what they believe. Then they get angry, feeling like failures, they persist even more.[31]

The efficacy of true faith, if found on planet earth, infinitely measures what the Lord said, "If you had faith of a grain of mustard seed, then you could say to this tree, pull yourself up by the root, and be planted by the sea; and it would obey you." This statement of the Lord, in response to the apostles asking for increase in faith, shows there is no understanding of true biblical faith. Christ, not yet crucified, buried, and resurrected spoke as a man of faith, to men lacking faith. Must we not only live by faith, but believe Christ is our faith. If the resurrection of Christ is false, then the Christian faith serves no purpose. We remain under judgment, and surely the wrath of God that comes upon children of disobedience.

The story is told of Jesus, upon entering into a village, and from a good way off seen by ten lepers who shouted, "Jesus, Master, have mercy on us." When he saw them, he said, "Go show yourselves unto the priests." They went to the priest, and along the way, supposedly healed of leprosy. Ten lepers cleansed as driving a car through a car wash.

One of them however, a Samaritan among nine Jews, when he saw that the leprosy healed turned back, and with a loud voice glorified God, fell down on his face at the feet of Jesus, and gave thanks. Jesus looked down and asked, "Were there not ten cleansed of leprosy; where are the other nine?" He very sorrowful said, "Arise, go your way, your faith made you well." The latter, in all probability went to the priest, but now with a testimony of the healing power of Christ. Will Christ find faith on return to planet earth? His people, the Jews, neglect to give thanks, and many still in original sin. What opportunity does the Gentile have to secure salvation?

Some say faith without works is dead. Wherein another may say, you have faith, I have works, show me faith without works, and I will show faith by my works. Who will know, if faith without works is dead, or alive? Those who go out of their way working for the Lord hold this verse as motive in ministry. Some even count their rewards along the way. Is that the manner for measuring Faith? The concluding verse about faith imputed on Abraham for his works, holds the truth. The body without the spirit is dead, so faith without works is just as dead. (Luke 17:6, 11-19; James 2:14-26)

Should you then rely on a teacher, pastor or even this book to grow the Faith of Christ? Upon retirement some twenty years, writing this book is a work of faith. Why, as a child do we remain dependent on the milk of the word? Some say an author should write as to those having less than the eighth grade. Others say an author should only write on things they know. God ordained the teacher and pastor to preach the word of the Lord, that the church not fail in its focus to nurture the young in faith, even unto the mature student.

A warning: The ministry as a work of God is not to learn how to be more like Christ, but to learn how to be in Christ; an abiding relationship. A teacher can stir up your mind and point you in the right direction, but only God can teach you the things of the Spirit unto understanding. Only in the Lord does one receive spiritual knowledge. The nurturing of the Word satisfy the needs of the soul, but the spirit needs to acknowledge and fulfill the will of God. The meaning behind the measure of Faith is to experience the Faith of Christ.

There is a difference between satisfaction and gratification. Pleasure, not intended to be the focus of our life or meaning behind existence, but pleasure is the function of the soul. Where there is no vision man casts off restraint in seeking worldly pleasures while attempting to walk in the Spirit. People begin to depart from values and godliness because their only focus is looking for ways to fill their emptiness with anything that gratifies the soul.

Gratification is the quenching of desire. When pleasure is the focus, emptiness is the result. When you pursue a pleasure and gratify that pleasure, your focus is gone and there is no measure left to the meaning of faith. The soul therefore, under construction taught of the Holy Spirit. The scripture is clear: be filled with the Spirit as in contrast to the works of the flesh in pursuing pleasure. (Gal. 4:16; Eph. 5:18)

An illustration, given of two men who went into the temple to pray: One sought gratification from pleasure, and while telling of his work of fasting twice a week, giving of tithes, he compared himself with one who would not lift his eyes toward heaven, but asking God to take mercy on a sinner. One is gratified through works, now empty, while the other justified

and exalted. What then, must one do to experience gratification in life? Jesus suggests, sell everything, give the proceeds
to the poor, and follow Him. Jesus remarked, "How difficult for
those with possessions to enter the Kingdom." It seems there
is no contradiction in works, but the condition to follow Jesus.
Where was he going, but to Calvary?

Who then are justified, and who are saved? The one who
asks for mercy, these are the justified. Jesus said, "Things,
which are impossible with men are possible with God."
Recall, He asked a blind man what he wanted. The man replied, "Lord, that I may receive my sight." With that, Jesus
said to him, "Receive your sight faith has made you well."
Upon which, followed the Lord. This is the way of salvation.
The people, seeing the result of such faith, gave praise unto
God.

Now then, when we look at the church, what is missing?
Is it not the Faith of Christ? There is no instruction on how to
follow the Lord. Many just believe by pretending that doubt
does not exist and whatever happens is just meant to be?
This is the talk of the fatalist. Surely, we are not so foolish,
having begun in the Spirit made perfect by the flesh. Many
formulate their own measures and then present them to God.
Mustering trust in human effort, expect God to act on their request. Faith is the gift of God, the impossible made possible,
meaning measurable by that gift of faith. (Gal. 3:3)

Further, faith is not of the flesh nor is it the result of any
human effort. No one should boast about his/her own faith.
Yet, how many times have you heard a Christian refer to their
faith as my faith? Those who use first party terms to define
faith likened to one standing in exaltation of their own works,
but be assured they are lowered to the very lowest.

This shows that they do not understand true faith. This
fabricated faith has no more power than a fly on a swatter.
Many Christians fold faith in their pocket book. Trusting in
money has certainly not proved to be valid: about as valid as

a rabbit's foot. It too has no measure or depth of meaning. The world of my will, will not change beyond my will to conquer my surroundings. This is not faith, but sheer effort. One cannot measure the meaning of faith beyond that of repeating the power of self-affirmation, a motivation of the flesh.

Mark Twain once stated that faith is belief in something you know is not so.[37] This definition for faith is created by effort. It has virtually nothing to do with the faith of Christ. All too many Christians live under a superstitious faith because they do not understand true faith. Biblical faith is the faith given us in good measure, pressed down by the Spirit of God so that we have the power to believe the word of God. Be obedient to His plan of salvation: faith without works is dead, but if you work out of a salvation of fear and trembling, you undermine the Word of God. God never does the work on behalf of your will, but God works in you according to His will, and does so of His good pleasure. (Phil. 2:12-13)

Faith lays aside the selfish life, so trust in God. We believe His word and His promises. Have faith in God and lay down your life knowing what God desires for you is much better than the desire of the world. God promises to satisfy us now, and rewards us in eternity. Now, that seems to me a fair means to measure faith. Now, contend for that faith.

Have you ever heard it said, "Since we love Him we keep His commandments?" We must look at the principles taught and not just pick out the commands that appeal to our human nature. The entire focus of this instruction is revealing to disciples and to us that we are to trust God. Is it His plan that we be successful, through our walk of faith? It is great to have set goals, as they give us focus and direction, but if the calling is of God, the destination is not readily revealed.

Many denominations insist, "Keep God's commandments." Surely they jest, or refer to the ten given Moses, and not the whole six hundred of Deuteronomy. If you abide in me, and my words abide in you, ask what you will as being done.

Herein, is the Father glorified. Bear fruit as the Bride of Christ, and reckon yourself dead unto the law. (Rom. 7:4)

The scripture teaches that a new creature in Christ will grow from the milk of the word, but we are also told that in order to gain spiritual maturity, we must eventually be taken off milk to chew upon the meat of the word. It is then that God teaches knowledge, building precept upon precept, little by little. God teaches the deeper things of the Spirit, but this will not occur unless taken off the milk. Many Christians give a testimony of salvation, but few give testimony from what they learn in the present. Even Pastors in a state of growth, need the meat of the Word. Growth comes by chewing on the meat of the Word of God; a satisfying, palatable savor.

Jesus said, "If you keep my commandments, you abide in my love; even as I have kept my Father's commandments, and abide in His love." This, from the lips of Jesus who at this time in history, was not yet glorified, spoke as the Son of Man. It was not until the resurrection that the enablement to abide spiritually in Christ Jesus was made possible. In keeping the commandments, they knew God, but in contrast, if the commandments were not kept, they knew not God. This was a simple test of knowledge. He/she who say, I know him and keep not his commandments, are liars, and the truth not in them. This is strong language, and it appears that to keep the commandments one must know the Lord on a personal level. The commandments come with the indwelling Spirit. If this is not so, then any person with a memory deficit could never be a Christian. (John 15:10; 1 John 2:3-6)

John the Apostle stood against Gnosticism, and spoke after the fact. Gnosticism was a religious movement finding its base in Christianity and Judaism. The movement, associated with mysticism, draws a thread of discussion connecting them to the concept of gnosis. Gnosis, a private kind of knowledge centered about the divine rather than faith, and associated with mysticism. Gnostic religious movements made extensive use of allegory and metaphors for interpreting biblical texts. The early church condemned their beliefs and practices though based on Christian and Jewish concepts. Their concept show matter as evil, and knowledge more important than faith.

This brings us to the next question, "If the Christian is dead unto the law, why the need to follow the commandments?" This opens the door to a number of denominations that say they obey the law and the commandments. If written on the heart of the believer, then the responsibility of the indwelling Holy Spirit is to bring to memory the words of Jesus. God the Father said through the letter to the Hebrews, "This is the promise that I will make with the house of Israel, I will put my laws into their mind, and write them in their hearts. I will be to them a God, and they shall be to me a people." (Heb. 8:10-13) Come now, let us reason, you must be born again, abiding in Christ in heavenly places is to know you are saved.

Now, let us consider the first letter of John. In this letter, many Christians believed they need to confess continually. Even though sin is covered by the blood, washed clean, separated from the law, and made the righteousness of God, need keep trucking on by confession upon confession. These things we write unto you, that your joy may be full. Think for a moment, John is advocating for the Christian message unto the Gnostics who believe matter is evil, and knowledge more important than faith. This then is the message:

*"Hearing of him, we declare to you, God is light, and in him, no darkness. If we say that we have fellowship with him, and walk in darkness, we lie, and do not the truth: But if we walk in the light, as he is in the light, we have fellowship one with another, and the blood of Jesus Christ his Son cleanses us from all sin. If we say that we have no sin, we deceive ourselves, and the truth is not in us. If we confess our sins, he is faithful and just to forgive our sins, and to cleanse us from all unrighteousness. If we say that*

*we have not sinned, we make him a liar, and his word is not in us."* (I John 1:5-10)

Can you detect the tone of the message? It is an explanation of a historical fact, not a command, something happened, and explained for others to learn through their testimony. The Gnostics determine their belief by sight, not by faith. They learn from another's experience. The message of John was not written to the believer, but about the believer, and not so much the need for salvation, but the need for testimony.

Born again, and raised together in Christ to heavenly places, we are not in the world to give testimony unto the Lord, but we are in Christ Jesus to give testimony unto the world. Discernment and understanding the deeper reason why things happen, clearly shows the deceitfulness of those attempting to keep the commandments, take this as a command. The believer's identity in Christ, confirms testimony of salvation, and through the faith of Christ, pressed down, running over, we testify to those who live by works of faith.

Upon confession, all sin forgiven, sin of the past: sin of the present: and sin of the future, all forgiven. Cleansed from all unrighteousness, the Christian now presented to God the Father, as holy, blameless, and without sin. Jesus paid the price through shedding of His blood on the cross. (1 John 1:4-10; Gal. 2:20; Eph. 1:4, 2:6; Col. 3:1-4)

Why then do we keep on sinning? Is it so that we may keep on confessing to keep the priest on the pay role? God forbid. How shall we, who are dead to sin, live any longer therein? Know you not, that as many as are placed into the death of Christ are buried with Him, and because of this state of occupancy in Christ, raised from the dead by the glory of the Father. Even so, we should walk in resurrected life. If, planted together in the likeness of His death, shall we not in the likeness of His resurrection, be glorified? Knowing this, that our old man is crucified with Him, that the body (whole mess of sin) might be destroyed, and from that day forward, no longer serve sin? He/she that is dead is free of sin. Now if we are dead with Christ, why is it so difficult to believe we live with Him in heavenly places?

We know that Christ, being raised from the dead, can never pass that way again, and for that matter, neither can the Christian. Death no longer dominates the Christian, no condemnation, no fear of wrath, and no judgment of God. With that, watch for His coming, day unto day with hope, faith, and love toward the brethren and humanity. (Rom. 6:1-10; 7:4)

Whatsoever we ask, we receive of Him, because we keep His commandments. When upon our heart and mind the written law is kept by the power of the Holy Spirit, we do those things that are pleasing in His sight. We know those who keep the commandments dwell in Him. We know that He abides in us, by the Holy Spirit, wherein He has given us as tutor, guide, and chooser of His will. We know to love the children of God, for when we love God, we know His commandments.

This is the love of God, know His appearing is near, even at the door. Precious are His promises who wills also to do them. Having the commandments written upon our hearts, there is no need to have them hang around the neck. Any deviation from the law, promptly reminded by the Spirit, and through the conscious advised of stepping out of His way, Truth, and Life, jump back without hesitation. (John 15:10; 1 John 1:9, 2:3 4; 3:22 24; 5:2)

This chapter showed how the meaning of faith, is measured by change. There is no doubt that many readers question what some passages revealed of the nature of God and man. This book, written to those who want a discerning look at why things happen, indicative by experience not as Gnostics seeking knowledge of the past, but in the presence of the truth. Only through the Faith of Christ, can one know the meaning and measure of faith. Saving faith is lost on planet earth. It grieves the Lord to know that upon His return,

He may not find saving faith on planet earth. Why is this a fact? Many have given up on His return.

It is not what we do, but who we are in Christ that counts. The next chapter develops a different sort of faith showing us hindrances to salvation, but He is patient and desires not that any should perish, but that all may come to Him for salvation. Even so, Lord Jesus, come.

Twentieth century technology opened the door to religious movements on planet earth. Religion is in plenteous supply, but Faith remains the question for the next chapter that describes various sorts of faith that hinders.

*"All too often, humanity becomes impatient with God, not giving heed to His Word."*

# CHAPTER TWO

# Sorts: The Type of Faith that Hinders

A *sort* of faith is a type of religion that hinders the Christian experience and testimony. Many religions now occupy planet earth. They come in droves, encircling the earth, hindering, persecuting, destroying the Christian Faith, and subjecting the Faithful in Christ to vain deceit and human philosophy. One must realize there is something terrible going on within the Christian mind. Mega churches, television ministries, community churches, and the denominational churches all seeking the wasted soul of humanity to reform, regenerate, and become members. The next few paragraphs reveal a number of these religious movements, and how they affect Christianity as a whole.

Over time, eight sorts of religious movements took root on planet earth. These, referred to as spiritual manifestations of God, began with Abraham. Religion came on the scene with Moses, then Krishna, Zorastor, Buddha, Christ, Mohammed, and Bahaullah. The latter's intent is to bring humanity under a One World Religious movement, a sign of the end times.

Beginning with the call upon Abram to go, and upon burying his father Terah at seventy-five years, departed from Ur of the Chaldees for the land of Canaan. A land God promised to all his descendents. God, changed the name of Abram to Abraham, meaning father of many nations, and made a promise to Abraham that his descendents would inherit the land of Canaan; the modern-day region of Israel, Palestine, Lebanon, and western part of Syria, as an everlasting covenant sealed with the sign of circumcision. Judaism, the religion of the Jew, is a manifestation representing the promises of God. It is through Judah, son of Jacob, who is the son of Isaac, son of Abraham that Jesus became the son of Mary, betrothed to Joseph. (Gen. 15:7; Luke 3-23)

Now that should have been the beginning and end for the linage of humanity. Accept the fact, the Lord brought Abram out from Ur of the Chaldees to give him the land of Canaan as an inheritance. However, who came along, but his father Terah, his nephew Lot, son of his brother Haran, and Sarai his wife. They all went forth from Ur of the Chaldees, to go into the land of Canaan. That was not in the plan of God.

All too often, humanity becomes impatient with God, not giving heed to His Word. The future of humanity came forth from other loins than Abraham. In particular, Sarah could not bear children, and under those circumstances, changed God's planning and had Abraham, now eighty-six, unite with Hagar their household maid. Hagar brought forth a son whose name was Ishmael.

Abraham, now one hundred years, Sarah conceived a son, named Isaac. His brother Ishmael is now fourteen years old. God reestablished His covenant, but they have a problem: What to do about Ishmael? In her spitefulness, Sarah told Abraham that her son Isaac would never be heir with his son Ishmael. Abraham, now totally frustrated, obliged to kick his first-born son Ishmael out of their home. However, God said to Abraham, "Let this not be so difficult, in all that Sarah has said, give heed unto her desire, for it is in Isaac that your seed shall prosper." That understood God told Abraham to take his second son Isaac; go into the land of Moriah and offer this seed of his posterity Isaac, as a burnt offering unto the Lord. Well, in obedience, Abraham rose up early the next morning, saddled his donkey, took two of his young men, Isaac his son with an armful of wood for a burnt offering, and went unto the place where God had told him. After all these circumstances, God wanted to test the faith of Abraham. Isaac questioned his father about the offering, upon which his father replied, "God will provide a lamb for the offering."

An interesting story about how God, at the very last second of time, prevented the sacrifice of Isaac. The forerunner of Christ Jesus, who for the purpose of saving humanity, was not so fortunate, but being found in the fashion of a man, humbled himself, and became obedient unto death, even the death of the cross. He brought about salvation of humanity.

Abraham, in a particular dispensation of time, was a spiritual manifestation; one of eight religious movements of our time worthy of mention. God made a promise with the condition of having children. Israel is evidence of the blessed seed of Abraham. Another was to inherit a specific parcel of land known as Israel. Not only was the blessing on Abraham to his seed, it extended to whosoever would appropriate that blessing as being a descendent of Abraham through faith.

The Christian, who rests in Christ, participates in the blessing of Abraham. We receive the blessing upon salvation. We, who are of the faith of Christ, are children of Abraham. Knowing that God would justify the Gentile through faith, said unto Abraham, "In you shall all the nations be blessed." The blessing of Abraham fell on the Christian Community by way of the cross. Cursed is every one that hangs on a tree: that the blessing of Abraham might fall on Gentiles, through Jesus Christ. This is not a hoax, but a matter of one English word, seed. Promises made to Abraham's seed, and that being Christ Jesus our Lord and Savior. Now, to Abraham and his seed were the promises made, not to many, but of one. Christian, if you are of Christ, then you are Abraham's seed, heir according to promise. That is why, as Christians, we are a blessing to humanity. Though many may deny this conclusion, it nevertheless is true. (Gen. 16:10-16, 17:19-21, 21:4-11, 22:1-3; Gal. 3:3-29; Phil. 2:8)

The second spiritual manifestation of sort revealed through Biblical context is that of Moses. His birth mother, fearful for his life, placed him in a woven basket of reeds, and put it in the river. 'Moses' is named 'saved him out of water' because of Pharaoh's daughter who then gave him to his mother for nurturing. Later, knowing the impossible situation of his kindred in slavery to the Pharaoh killed one of Pharaoh's taskmasters. Moses fled from Pharaoh to the land of Median. Later, while tending the flock of Jethro, his father-in-law and Priest of Median, the Angel of the Lord appeared to him from the midst of a burning bush, a spiritual manifestation.

God gave him to understand, he was to recover and restore his kindred from the land of Egypt. An oath, given as a promise, carried out by placing the blood of a lamb on each doorpost and lintel of his/her place of dwelling. God was about to put an end to all  first born of Egypt, but in so doing, had to alert the Angel from putting an end to the first born of the seed of Israel living on the same street as Egyptians.

Now, the faith of Moses is also that of promise, and similar to the blessing of Abraham, a continuum. The Passover, and established as an everlasting ordinance for Israel. This act of deliverance, celebrated each year in August, is the second spiritual manifestation of God. (Ex. 2:10-11. 3:3-6)

Some sorts of religious movements seeking recognition are without scriptural reference. The religious manifestation of Krishna began with the incarnation of Vishnu.[6] He is one of three gods found in the Hindi triad, the official language of northern India. Traced back some two hundred years before Christ, Krishna became popular among the Avatars. The incarnation of a Hindu deity, who in human or animal form, is worshipped in India. (The movie of the twenty-first century, showed an Avatar, as savior. Christians watched in awe.)

In the fifteenth century, a revival launched by Chaitanya, a Bengalese devotee of the god Vishnu, emerged on the scene. He claimed to be the incarnation of Krishna. In July 1965, one named Prabhpada formed the first International Society for Krishna consciousness. Greenwich Village, New York, the message of Krishna became entrenched in the hippie movement. The faith of Krishna a sort of mysticism, and manifested by the Hare Krishna Religious Movement.

Another sort of spiritual manifestation, and not supported by scripture, is Zoroastrian.[7] Coined from teachings of a Persian prophet Zoroaster. He worshiped wisdom and the religion of good. According to scholars, Zoroastrianism was the first religion to believe in angels, a day of judgment, Satan, and the ongoing battle between good and evil. These ideas influenced the development of Judaism, Christianity, and Islam. The Zoroastrians, recognized in the Western world as that of being the Magi, and visited the infant Jesus. The faith of Zoroaster is a sort of universal wisdom of humanity.

Yet another sort of spiritual manifestation, and having a grip on humanity, is the divine manifestation of the Buddha.[8] It began in India around 566 BC. He saw sickness, old age, death, and was influenced by a monk in rags thought, "I shall be like him." Six years he meditated eating only roots, leaves and fruit, and in the end, supposedly gained ancient wisdom and understood all things.

The Buddha taught as one having two natures. An ordinary nature made up of feelings such as fear, anger, jealousy, and that of a true nature, pure, wise, and perfect. He taught how we, among plants, trees, and all things living consist all around us, as everything. Truth, determined by change, and due to cause and effect, brings about good *karma*.[10] The law of karma, says, "For every event that occurs, there will follow another event whose existence was caused by the first, and this second event will be pleasant, or unpleasant according if its cause is skillful or unskillful. In other words, what comes around goes around.

Karma is deserving of happening. We receive what we earn, whether good or bad. We are the way we are due to things done in the past. Thoughts and actions determine the kind of life we have, and every moment of every day, we create new karma in what we say, do, and think, as reality. We need not fear karma. It is our friend. It teaches us to create a brighter, safer, and prosperous future. This sort of faith could be the intent of Buddha, and karma the experience.

More recently, and without scriptural reference, in 612 A.D. Mohammed experienced some sort of a divine manifestation. He, according to literature, received a call from the Angel Gabriel. This call initiating his career as the Prophet of Allah, the Apostle of Arabia, and founder of Mohammedanism.[9] In his fortieth year, on his last visit to the City of Mecca, Mohammed died of a terrible fever.

Mohammedanism wants to be a world power and a universal religious movement. According to the latest accounts, there are currently over 300 million in the world. The principles, all contained in the Koran for Mohammedanism, the prophets of Islam, are of Arabian, Judaism, Christianity, and Zoroastrian interpretation. The doctrines of Islam are essentially those of the Bible, but without contextual reference. The devil, known as Iblis was very close to God, but cast out of heaven for not paying homage to Adam. Judgment precedes resurrection. Signs in heaven and on earth, identify with those of the New Testament, and extend to all living creatures.

It is interesting to note that upon death, all men have a mansion requiring 80,000 servants to administer their need. Each has seventy-two wives, each having perpetual youth, beauty, and vitality. The faith of Mohammed comes under the guise of some sort of fetish or magical phenomenon.[7]

This research opened the door to many different sorts of faith, but among the most significant are those that slipped through the cracks of the church without notice. Considered as insignificant to the Christian view, but they have a strong influence on Christianity by taking on the Church role, and claim to be the modern day savior of the world. Discussion on this religious movement is threatening to the church at large, but if the truth were known, many members of your particular denomination will endorse The Baha'i World Faith.

Dr. Walter Martins, Christian Research Foundation, indexed the King James Version of the Bible as, The Cults Reference Bible. He shows the faith of the Baha'i as having unique relevance to the modern world, and to the Christian faith. In addition to Martin's work, are references from the Internet, articles written in defense and the indifferent, leading to a thought provoking discussion on the Baha'i World Faith.

When seeking relations, the Baha'i World Faith has difficulty in reaching the population, for the Bahai cannot accept teachings contrary to reason, nor pretend to believe teachings they cannot understand, of which the Christian accepts many. To that end considered superstition rather than true religion. This supports Paul's statement to the Ephesians, "Having their understanding darkened, they are alienated from the Life of God through the ignorance that is in them, because the heart is blind." Most, if not all, religious movements of this sort fall under the definition of pretense. How then, do we contend for the Faith of Christ? (Eph. 4:18)

Christianity always held the predominant position of faith in North America, and Europe. In all fairness, the Baha'i have similar life principles. According to the Newsletter, the Baha'i World Faith International Community, they provide the promise of world peace. This has been the dream of Christianity for years, particularly within the Roman Catholic Church whose vision is to secure world peace in preparation for the return of Christ on planet earth. In a letter from the Universal House of Justice, Haifa, Bahai reads in part:[3]

There is a Great Peace movement towards which people of good will throughout the centuries have inclined their hearts, expressed their vision, underlying the promises of the sacred scriptures to mankind, and now at long last within the reach of the international community. For the first time in history, it is possible for everyone to view the entire planet, with its diversified peoples, with one perspective. World peace is not only possible, but also inevitable in bringing about the evolution of planet earth, "The planetization of mankind".

Planetization is not in the dictionary. It does sound however, like a plan for a One World Religion. This overall world plan, necessary for completing a new One World Order, could come in the next decade. The Baha'i World Faith, foremost in the structure for world peace, sits in the doorway of the United Nations to influence the world.[4] Few Christians sit in protest one way or another.

Doctrines of this sort of a Divine Manifestation, is the central plank of the Baha'i theology.[5] Throughout their doctrine, Baha'is are able to take favorable doctrinal positions with members of major world religions. Each of their founders believe these instances of visitation, manifests those of God. Each religion has a measure of divine truth. We have already itemized these spiritual manifestations of faith. In review, they are: Abraham, Moses, Krishna, Zoroaster, Buddha, Christ, Mohammed, and Bahaullah. Each manifestation is a complement to the other. Bahaullah, is the most supreme manifestation of the current church age, and includes those followers of Christ, Judaism, and Christianity.

Understand these sorts of spiritual manifestations do not pose a threat, or a conflict with the Christian faith. After all, most believe there is but one Lord, one Faith, one Baptism, and therefore one God as Father of all. Notice, it is the faith of Baha'i, and not of Christ wherein faith upon planet earth, is established. The Bahai took the task of fulfilling the need to restore a spiritual agenda, principles necessary for social regeneration, and the attainment of one worldwide religion.

Baha'is brush aside the Christian emphasis on personal faith, and the regeneration process as means for global salvation. Unfortunately, this book takes the position that the

Faith of Christ is lost on Planet Earth. Notice in both religions, Christian and Bahai, the emphasis placed on faith, is that faith of the founders, Christ and Bahaullah. The emphasis placed in this book is on the Faith of Christ, with the intent to show the readers the need, not for a personal faith of their choosing, but the need for appropriating the Faith of Christ. (Eph. 4:5)

The Baha'i Faith is rationalistic. They rely wholly on reason, an attribute of the mind, as guide for their belief system. They do not accept teaching contrary to reason, but rather interpret characteristics of truth allegorically, by symbolism to illustrate biblical doctrines as the Holy Trinity, the bodily Resurrection of Christ, the existence of angels, evil spirits, and doctrines of heaven and hell. They deny that man fell through Adam from his original spiritual and moral state. Sin is but a characteristic of the lower, baser morality of nature, wherein education brings deliverance. There is no value in Christ's sacrificial death on the cross. Yet, given all the above and more, the Baha'i cry for a one-world religion insist they are in complete harmony with the Christian Faith. In this way, they infiltrate the Christian Church with literally no resistance whatsoever.

The Baha'i, active across the globe, have a total membership of over 5 million persons. This sort of rationale of numbers reflects the need for Christian discernment. The Christian must understand the difference between reason and faith. We have weapons, not of this world, but mighty through God to pull down these strongholds of reason. Any figment of the imagination, (thought) inconsistent with the knowledge of God (Word) and brought into captivity to the obedience of Christ, will upon obedience to act, punished to the uttermost. Please, reckon this as so! (2 Cor. 10:4-6)

This sort of rational faith, cause Christians to fall away from the church, hindering and even destroying the Christian belief system. Fortunately, the situation affects the time line for the era of Christianity on Planet Earth. There must be a falling away before revealing a man of sin. He who opposes and exalts himself above all called of God and worshipped, so he, pretending to be God may sit in the temple of God, showing himself as God. (2 Thes. 2:3-4)

This chapter considered in brief, eight divine manifestations of rationale. Some Christian, while others represent the son of perdition, a child of Satan who drives the Christian to absolute despair. Wherein, the Christ is the divine spiritual manifestation of Christianity. He is runner up to Bahaullah founder of Baha'i World Faith. If as Christian, we accept even in part, any of the latter five religious movements to be more than information, the author of this book is in danger of bordering on heresy. This chapter, if it contained the full explanation and description of these many sorts of divine manifestations, it would exceed one thousand pages. That is why referenced material is available for research.

Many faiths infiltrate the Christian Church. With so many different versions of the Bible that put the Word of God in competition one with the other, the true Word of God is lost on Planet Earth. Each version, as translated for the modern thinking believer and unbeliever add, delete, insert words, and prepositions to alter and change the historical meaning, context, and commentary of an original Word of God. The original, by the way, is not available anywhere on Planet earth. Each translation is the copy of a copy, and open to interpretation.

A significant reason for appropriating the Faith of Christ is to connect with the power of the resurrection. A Christian must believe, must rightly divide, and must discern the Word of God to be set apart from false teaching. How can we trust the Bible when there appears to be so many translations?

The scripture teaches that the Holy Spirit indwelling in man, and inspired of Almighty God, gives understanding. This confirms all scripture, given by inspiration of God, is profitable for doctrine, reproof, correction, instruction, and righteousness. Why, that we may know Christ in the power of resurrection, the fellowship of his sufferings, conformable unto His death? If by any means, we attain the resurrection of the dead, this power keeps us in the Faith of Christ without which, there is no hope. We being the dead in sin, but now alive in Christ, a brand new creature. (Job 32:8; Phil. 3:10-11; 2 Tim. 3:16)

The next chapter, thresholds of faith, intensifies the need to go back to the Bible. Interpretation demands we compare scripture with scripture. The intent is to learn what really divides Christianity, is it animal or mineral? The Bible, clear on teaching unity of the faith, intensifies the endeavor to keep the unity of the Spirit in the bond of peace. (Eph. 4:3)

*"Most Christians do not have a problem with the power of God, but with the Word of God."*

# CHAPTER THREE

# Threshold:
# The Inferences of Faith

In the preceding chapter, we learned movements of religion begin with some form of esoteric charisma initiated by some spiritual presence with such intensity it materializes into a spiritual manifestation. A mystery confined and understood only by the founders who organized it, as religious worship.

The threshold of faith, as the intensity of a religious experience, is a measure of spiritual experience. An action produces a response from people of faith, group, or denomination. The intensity of experience measures the Life of Christ in a Christian. The Bible declares Christ is our life, and faith is that measure of eternal life, a gift according as God has dealt to every person, that measure of faith. (Rom. 12:3, Eph. 4:7, Col. 3:4, Heb. 11:1)

Now, this is effectual reasoning. Many a Christian has never questioned what it means to follow Christ, rather wanting to be like Jesus. The former is possible, the latter impossible. Jesus said, "If anyone desires to come after me, let them deny himself, take up the cross daily, and follow me. For whosoever desires to save, his life will lose it, but whosoever loses his life for my sake will save it." (Luke 9:23-24)

This again, is effectual reasoning. What does it mean, "... whosoever loses his life for my sake will save it." A Christian bears the cross of Christ in humility and grace, not around their neck as a piece of jewelry, but in recognition of their death on the cross. The essence of the verse is to lose your life and then to revive your life and live again. A Christian must follow Jesus, but with such intensity, that he/she wills death.

Jesus said, "He that hears my word, and believes on Him that sent me, has everlasting life, and shall not come into condemnation; but is passed from death unto life." Notice the condition; "on Him" not "in Him" as the devil believes. The preposition "on" relates to the condition that we must trust the Father that He sent Jesus to be sin for us. This is a prerequisite to knowing, we pass from death unto life. We love our brothers and sisters in the Lord, because, if we do not love our brother, we have not passed over Jordan, but remain in Egypt. Later in this chapter, the lyrics depicting this scenario, written for enjoyment. (John 5:24; 2 Cor. 5:21; 1 John 3:4)

There is the mystery behind the gospel. What does it mean to experience death unto salvation? The analogy of the Jordan River shows life. The Word of God is so powerful that without realizing what is happening, one passes through death unto life. This is similar to crossing the Red Sea and later the Jordan River. This is the threshold of faith. Except for the noise, passing over just happens. Who knows when a tree falls in the forest, if there is no one to hear the noise? Looking back, there is no evidence of the past, except in memory.

This is the true meaning of the term, born again. "For the word of God is quick, and powerful, and sharper than any two edged sword, piercing even to the dividing asunder of soul and spirit, and of the joints and marrow, and is a discerner of the thoughts and intents of the heart." The Word of God is a living entity, powerful, sharper than a sword, dividing soul and spirit, even the joints and marrow of flesh, discerning thoughts and intents of life itself. (Heb. 4:12)

The wording is not explicit. Most Christians do not have a problem with the power of God, but with the Word of God. It should not be necessary to change the wording, structure, or style of scripture to fit the meaning of those who translate the scripture. The power of God makes the Word of God come alive in the Christian. In the last chapter, we answered the question, "How can we trust the Word of God when there are so many Bible translations?" The scripture teaches that the Spirit dwelling in man, inspired of God, gives understanding. Thus confirming all scripture, as inspired of God, is profitable for doctrine, reproof, correction, instruction, and righteousness.

Paraphrasing is the attempt to make the Word of God simple to understand, and to impress the meaning intended. The text is a restatement of the original, a method for teaching and studying the Word of God. This book contains a number of paraphrased verses to improve understanding, but the intent of the author is not to change the meaning. As a caution, research the references and confirm the scriptures.

The Old Testament prepared the way of the New Testament. It did not lay the foundation for the New Testament, only prepared the way. A foundation is something upon which to build. A structure is but an assemblage of walls, cabinetry, ceiling, and roof. This chapter lays open the threshold of faith, calling for clarification of scripture.

The previous passage of scripture (Heb. 4:12) uses the term asunder as a divider of soul and spirit. The online dictionary defines "asunder" as an adverb, adjective, tearing something into pieces to the point of shredding. Dividing "asunder" the soul, spirit, and body means the Christian is tripartite, or one consisting of three parts, a trichotomy. The Old Testament describes this immaterial part of humanity as a dichotomy, consisting of two, body and soul/spirit. Interpreting meaning from Old Testament passage to New Testament is often the wrong application for Christians indwelt by the Holy Spirit. Transferring two parts for three, what do you have, five. Unless there is a dividing asunder, of one making two, it is meaningless. New Testament application is a challenge for Old Testament personalities. The make up of soul and spirit requires accessing a different threshold of faith.

It is not the intent to divide the threshold of faith, because the Book of Hebrews refers to many personalities in the Old Testament as having faith. Where then is the righteousness of God revealed from faith to faith? The just shall live by faith. The law, in the sight of God justifies no man, and it is evident: The just shall live by faith, whether through an Old Testament personality, or a New Testament Christian. (Rom. 1:17; Gal. 3:11)

Could it be the Holy Spirit did not dwell in Old Testament personalities? The Holy Spirit obviously moved upon persons for a specified reason and time, but it seems there is sufficient reason to doubt the reality of the Holy Spirit in Old Testament personalities. In most personalities of the Old Testament, the Holy Spirit was not the guide and comforter, as apparent to the New Testament Christian. So, just how did the Lord work in Old Testament personalities, and why is there no indication of the fallen nature of man in spirit?

The Lord appeared to, spoke to Abraham, Isaac, Solomon, Moses, Aaron, Gideon, Menorah, father of Samson, David, Solomon, Zachariah, father of John the Baptist, Joseph, espoused husband of Mary, Mother of Jesus, and on the road to Damascus, Paul, the Apostle. Upon what threshold is faith inferred? It appears from the text that the Lord appeared in visible form, out of which He spoke.

This text, "The Lord Appeared Unto" taken from a key word search, appears in the King James Version of The Bible. The search brought out twenty-three results. There are many inferences that speak of God working in Old Testament personalities, but the intent is to show the absence of the term 'Holy Spirit' in describing these events.

Absence confirms that the Holy Ghost, though recognized as the third person of the Godhead, was not involved with humanity. His involvement happened after the resurrection of Jesus Christ. While the earth was under construction, without from, void, and in darkness, the Spirit moved upon the face of the deep, the face of the water. It seems He was more involved with physical matter and transparent energy than information about the threshold of faith.

Many Old Testament personalities testify of having faith. Yet the term 'faith' is mentioned only twice in searching the King James text of the Old Testament, but referenced is made to many as having faith. He said: "I will hide My face from them, I will see what their end will be, For they are a perverse generation, Children in whom is no faith." Further, "Behold, his soul which is lifted up is not upright in him: but the just shall live by **His** faith." (Deut. 32:20; Hab. 2:4)

Notice the pronoun **His.** This is a direct prophecy concerning the faith of Christ wherein whose faith the just should live. Herein lay the problem. The righteousness of God revealed from Old Testament personalities to recipients of faith in New Testament personalities. The just shall live by faith that the law in sight of God justifies no man. It is therefore evident the just shall live by faith, and not by works. Look at the proud, their soul is not right, but the just and righteous shall live by **His** faith and in the faithfulness of Christ, **His** faithfulness. (Hab. 2:4; Rom. 1:17; Gal. 3:10-12; Heb. 10:38)

There is a curious passage in the body of Jewish civil and religious law.[32] It suggests that Moses gave six hundred directives to the Israelites. David reduced them to eleven in Psalm 15. Isaiah reduced these eleven to six Chapter 33:15. Micah 6:8 reduced them to three; and Isaiah 56:1 to two. Amos 5:4 summed these six hundred directives to one. Does this not substantiate, support, prove, validate, confirm, solidify, make real, give form and substance to the fact that Habakkuk condensed them to just one formidable, highly impressive prophecy, "The just shall live by **HIS FAITH**?"

This threshold of faith, in all good conscience, questions the statement, "Will Christ find faith when He returns to planet earth," There is reason to believe, He will not find faith, but not willing that any should perish, His patience enduring, some people may yet experience His faith on planet earth.

Let us assume, since Jesus Christ, in the Person of the Holy Spirit abides in our spirit, His faith by position then revealed through the Spirit. The personality, that part of the soul consisting of mind, emotion, and will, and in the process of transformation, not enabled as a faith generator. With that in mind consider, "But if the Spirit of Him that raised up Jesus from the dead dwell in you, He that raised up Christ from the dead shall also revitalize your mortal bodies by His Spirit that dwells in you." This concludes that faith by position, generated through the power of the Holy Spirit as the Faith of Christ. (Gen. 2:7; Rom. 8:11, 12:2)

The soul is yet learning of its place in the body. However, the old nature Adam, who hung out in the human spirit and placed into Christ's death, died on the cross. The nature of Adam, the old man, is now dead and buried. A new spiritual creation enters upon the scene, the 'born again' Christian. A new creature, but because of its spiritual characteristics, abides in heaven in Christ Jesus. (Rom. 3:6, 8:7; Eph. 2:6)

Resurrected together with Christ, this new creature, made as the righteousness of God in Christ Jesus, is no longer on planet earth. The new man rose as a brand new entity, alive and clothed in Christ Jesus. Not abiding in an earthly tent, we wait for a new incorruptible, perfect body like that of Christ. Can you understand how wild that is? The Bible tells us that even our wildest imagination there is no measure by which when fully redeemed, we are whole. Meanwhile, God made Christ our Life, Wisdom, Righteousness, Sanctification, and Redemption. It is only by the Faith of Christ wherein we now stand, can we even access such Grace. Rejoice therefore in this hope, the Glory of God. (Rom. 5:2; 1 Cor. 1:30, 2 Cor. 5:21; Eph. 2:6; Gal. 2:20; Col. 3:4)

Again, in confirmation, where is this new creation? The new creature, made in the image of Christ abides in heavenly places in Christ Jesus. The simplicity of this scripture when taken literally shows the purity and richness of God's Grace to the believer. Looking back, it took twenty-five years of Grace before the Lord revealed this mystery of the gospel to the author; taught under the rule of 'all things positional' church, misled. The threshold of faith, infers coming of age, maturity of the believer, whereas many are children lost.

Let us now go back a paragraph or two and learn just how to follow Christ in His death, burial, and resurrection. Recall, (Luke 9:23-24) Jesus said, "If anyone desires to come after me, let them deny him/her self, take up the cross daily, and follow me. For whosoever desires to save, his/her life will lose it, but whosoever loses life for my sake will save it?"

If anyone desires, that is reckons on the truth and power of the Word of God to deny him/her self, and take up the cross daily and follow Jesus, is saved. Adam, listened to the Devil, denied allegiance to God, and became ritually died. He exchanged the image of God in spirit for the image the Devil in spirit. As born of Adam, all have sinned and come short of the Glory of God. Jesus said to the Jews, "You are of your father, the devil." As followers of Christ crucified, buried, resurrected, and ascended, we need no longer battle in the flesh. Given over to the Holy Spirit, we are free from bondage of sin and the Devil. (John 8:44; Rom. 3:23; Gal. 5:17, 1 John 5:21)

How should we then walk?[12] Though we walk in the flesh, we are not at war with the flesh. We no longer bear allegiance to the old man, for it is Christ who lives in us: and the life we live in the flesh, we live by the faith of the Son of God, who loved us, gave Himself for us. The experience of salvation intensifies as we apply passages of scripture that reflect who we really are in Christ Jesus, not on what we were in Adam. No longer sinners in need of salvation, but saints, faithful in Christ. (Gal. 2:20; 2 Cor. 10:3; Eph. 1:1)

We bring your attention to the application of salvation as it relates to physical death. A most beautiful song, written to comfort and assure the elderly of life after death, but denies the efficacy of the cross on the living. The song, "I won't have to cross Jordan alone," by Thomas Ramsey and Charles E. Durham, reminds one of the cross, but not one to the cross. The lyrics suggest an internment:

> *When I come to the river at the ending of day*
> *When the last winds of sorrow have blown;*
> *There'll be somebody waiting to show me the way*
> *I won't have to cross Jordan alone.*

> *I won't have to cross Jordan alone*
> *Jesus died all my sins to atone;*
> *In the darkness I see he'll be waiting for me*
> *I won't have to cross Jordan alone.*

> *Often times I'm weary and troubled and sad*
> *When it seems that my friends have all flown;*
> *There is one thought that cheers me and*
> *makes my heart glad,*
> *I won't have to cross Jordan alone.*

> *I won't have to cross Jordan alone*
> *Jesus died all my sins to atone;*
> *In the darkness I see he'll be waiting for me*
> *I won't have to cross Jordan alone.*
> *Though the billows of trouble and sorrow may sweep*
> *Christ the Saviour will care for his own;*
> *Till the end of my journey my soul he will keep and*
> *I won't have to cross Jordan alone.*

> *I won't have to cross Jordan alone*
> *Jesus died all my sins to atone;*
> *In the darkness I see he'll be waiting for me*
> *I won't have to cross Jordan alone.*

The song depicting the Crossing of Jordan, an analogy of physical death. Jesus is the Way, the Truth, and the Life. No one comes unto the Father except through Him. (John 14:6) It is only as we appropriate the Faith of Christ do we cross over Jordan. This Threshold of Faith, in which we come into the promise land, is literally the Eternal Life of Christ, but to some, just a position of grace. Thanks be to God, this is not an internment, a stay of execution, but the literal reality of the resurrected life found in Christ Jesus.

A stay of execution occurs when a someone decides that an individual, upon accepting Jesus Christ as personal savior, is not really saved until the church executive files new evidence to the contrary, or one progressively matures in a positional union with Christ. At the time of salvation, they reason, the believer enters into a union with Jesus Christ, that is coincidentally, a stay of execution.

The Christian is placed in Christ through a mode known as the Baptism of the Holy Spirit. Experiencing union with Christ is like a revival at a  camp meeting. Many, in agreement believe Christian is in Christ; a new creature; a new birthday; born again; and with a new human spirit; and has the right to fellowship with God. Union with Christ, confirmed by water baptism without the Faith of Christ, is an initiation 'right' for church membership.

Most new translations of the Bible, in defining how one becomes a child of God, use the terms right and authority. Only in the older translations is the term 'power' used to define how the Christian experiences the Grace of God. It is by Grace we are saved through faith and not of works should any boast. The term 'right' is conforming to law, the term 'authority' imposed by others, whereas the term 'power' is an action of the will. Accordingly, Christ created the world according to His will. God's will exerts power on things invisible to bring about things visible. The term 'right' infers ownership. One does not demand anything belonging to God. Faith is not a right, but of Grace. (Eph. 2:8; Rom. 1:20)

It is not for us to understand the how of things that happen. When we get to where we are going, these will be revealed. As it was with Abraham, God told him to go to a place that would be shown him in due time. Why should we expect anything different? For by Him were all things created, that are in heaven, and that are in earth, visible and invisible, whether they be thrones, or dominions, or principalities, or powers: all things were created by Him, and for Him. Who is the image of the invisible God, and who is the firstborn of every creature? Is it not of Christ, by whom things in heaven come created, and on earth, visible and invisible, whether they be thrones, or dominions, or principalities, or powers: all things were created by Him, and for Him. He is before all things, and by Him all things consist. He is the head of the body, the church: who is the beginning, the firstborn from the dead; that in all things He might have the preeminence. It pleased the Father that in Him all fullness indwells. (Col. 1:15-19)

Now, that being said, how can anyone say, "I want to be like Christ." What they are saying, knowingly or unknowingly, "I want to be like God." The New Age movement, and the Church of Jesus Christ of the Latter Day Saints, the Mormon Church, and others want to be little gods of their own making. The founder, Joseph Smith claims to be a descendent of Christ.[36] The New Age movement's hope is unite all into a one world religion. This encompasses a wide range of religions from spirit worship, Eastern mysticism, Mind-science religion, and psychology. Its purpose is to discover the god-within. People need look no further for answers to life. Everything one needs to know is already there.[38]

Reader, do you really want to be like Christ, or even more like Christ? Now you know where to go, but not where you are going, because, in all likelihood, it may not be heaven! This is certainly not the threshold of saving faith, but an inference of a sort of faith. Let none deceive you with vain words, vanity of reason, for because of these things the wrath of God comes upon all the children of disobedience. Do you qualify, or even want to? (Eph. 2:2. 5:6)

Further to becoming children of disobedience, a behavioral condition exists resulting in more confusion. The believer's position in Christ is secure, and the righteousness of God, imputed, yet our condition in Christ, while resting on moral behavior, is often far from perfect. God, by accepting us as positional, then must continue to work tirelessly, to bring our condition into agreement with position. This indicates our salvation is incomplete. There must be more than this!

How often does the scripture teach, salvation is complete in Christ? Many, many times for, "We are complete in Him, who is head of all principality and power." If complete, then why waste time in suggesting more? The moment we trust the Lord Jesus to save us, are we still in an imperfect condition?

Having a perfect position, we are no better than a sinning, arrogant Christian. The righteousness of God, based on the Lord Jesus Christ and made sin on the cross, though judicially perfect before God, and accepted in the Beloved, not yet in Christ; even being made the righteousness of God in Him? Having security by position, we continue to search diligently seeking new ways, new bibles, and new means to live in disobedience. Christian, this is bad behavior. (2 Cor. 5:21; Eph. 1:6, 5:18; Col. 2:10)

If we originally trusted the Lord Jesus to save us, but if imperfect, then what must we do to be truly saved? Even having a perfect position, we remain but a sinner saved by Grace. All the righteousness of God, all the blood shed on the cross to bear our sin, past, present, and future is wasted. A Christian, accepted in the Beloved does not practice sin. Counseling with the Mind of Christ, the behavior coming to the surface most frequently was lack of assurance. (1 John 5:21)

Carrying on now, and on behalf of those lacking assurance, a new religious movement eventually comes along. In the eye of the beholder, is truly a new manifestation of the spirit of holiness. In the previous chapter, a number of these spiritual manifestations emerged on planet earth, the latest among them, the Baha'i World Faith. Since then Churches, by modifying the doctrine of salvation to suit opened the door to false teaching fitting of all spiritual experience. One in particular, the Bahai World Faith Movement, invites those Christians lacking assurance, to enter their gate over which the threshold is but an inference of faith.

The founder of the Baha'i Faith, Baha'u'llah, born in Persia, November 12, 1817, and at the age twenty-seven, began an undertaking that gradually captured the imagination of every race, culture, class, and nation on planet earth. Baha'u'llah claimed to be the Messenger of God to this generation, the bearer of Divine Revelation. Even, the promises of God given to Abraham, Isaac, and Jacob, once applicable only to Israel, now apply to all people of Planet Earth.

This means that rationalized systems, preserved within traits of earlier types of authority, show the principle figures as having control over the direction of the movement. Christian movements, predicated on the office of Jesus Christ, have no jurisdiction over that of divine manifestations.[15] That being the case, denominations emerging after the fact can claim authority, or have special significance unavailable to others entitling them to demand obedience by membership.

Charismatic authority based on bonding between authority figures and followers highly emotional in nature. Devotion, action on the part of followers stem from a trust often blind and fanatical. This makes the bond very strong when it is working, but if the emotion fades, the bond breaks down and acceptance of the legitimacy of authority can disappear.

Such are religious movements that allow freedom of spiritual expression, manifested by the sound of musical instruments, and clothing that draw attention to those of the opposite gender, and of the same gender to participate in dance, the chant, and the beating of drums, despicable practice of faith. This chapter brought out a number of Biblical passages that support the factual translation of older versions of scripture.

It seems people, emotionally drawn toward thresholds with inferences of faith, easily deceived. They display their faith with clarity and utterance, through music, and lyrics of the world more so, than by the inspired Word of God. This book reveals a number of religious movements coming on the scene disrupting traditional church practice. It is with that thought, we move on to the next chapter: Pattern and Frequency of faith to come upon Planet Earth.

*"It is hard to accept failure, but even harder to confess failures to God."*

# CHAPTER FOUR

# Pattern: Frequency of Faith to Come Upon Planet Earth

There is a misconception that when we believe there is a pretence that doubt does not exist, and whatever we believe will surely happen. Many formulate their own plans and then present them to God, muster up faith of their own delight by human effort, and then expect God to act accordingly. As mentioned earlier many Christian lack assurance and doubt their salvation experience. Of such comes a departure from the faith. (1 Tim.4:1)

This chapter will show how different religious movements frequent the marketplace in search for patterns of faith open to change. One that comes immediately to mind is the word Chrislam. A Christian television personality who brings to Christians the frequency of faith coming upon planet earth in these latter days. Chrislam, a combination of Christianity and Islam indorsed by some church leaders. Including the author of The Purpose Driven Life.

There is good material in the book, but in my opinion, it is somewhat misleading. It consists of more psychological motivation than Christian directive. One has made an allegory of placing one drop of sewer water into a gallon of milk, and asking if you would take a drink. The obvious answer is, of course not, but this pattern of faith is becoming frequent, and deceiving the babe in Christ and even the mature Christian.

Those in the Ecumenical Movement are preparing the apostate world to receive the system of Antichrist. An apostate is one who abandoned their Christian faith. Some modern evangelicals in replacing love for truth, compromise the holiness of God. Such proponents are in league with those planning the one world government. It takes a bit of charisma to set up a true pattern of worship fitting to all, but the Ecumenical Movement has many prominent supporters.

In keeping with the theme of this book, "The Faith of Christ Jesus, Lost on Planet Earth" and "Pattern: Frequency of Faith coming upon Planet Earth," the next few paragraphs may be hard to digest. The Salvation Army is a community of believers known as Salvationists. Para-church in practice, their creed follows the doctrine of the Methodist. Armenian by tradition, one exception, they do not practice the sacraments of baptism and communion. This lack brings them by way of definition, a Para-Church organization.

The Salvation Army began as a Christian Mission in East London. Founded in 1865 by William and Catherine Booth, they established its mandate as an army of volunteers. William Booth, one day dictating a letter casually mentioned their mission was like an army of volunteers. Bramwell Booth, his son rejecting the term, caused his father to change the term to "salvation." Thus the name stands today as, The Salvation Army. Known for its rigidity in conduct, William and Catherine modeled their mission in the style and color of an army regiment, complete with uniform, drum, trumpets, and the flag.

William, of course, was General, while pastoral leaders were Envoys, Lieutenants, Captains, Majors, right up to Brigadier General. Laypersons were Salvationists. As of 2012, the Salvation Army operates in 125 countries, providing services in 175 different languages.[1] The Christian Mission concept carried over to the Salvation Army, caring for the poor and outcasts of London. Similar in pattern and frequency, but one not so Christian, the Baha'i World Faith.[1] With a population of six million, and operating in more than many countries, makes the Army a bag of small potatoes.

The Salvation Army gains its financial support from different churches, social, and community gatherings. Catherine was the advocate for the poor, and responsible for soliciting funds from the wealthy to the elite. In today's Army, the female officer is often responsible for finance. The Army's community approach, as initiated in London, follows the same pattern throughout the world. Serving soup to the hungry, soap for washing the body, and salvation for the soul; soup, soap, and salvation, as an acronym, "The three 'S's'. In most corps, hearing the gospel of salvation must come first, followed by soup and soap.

Because of their approach, most who come for aid are the alcoholic, drug addict, prostitute, and the down and outer. The British, struggling under the weight of the Industrial Revolution, drank alcohol to epidemic proportions. The "Gin" epidemic of the eighteenth century, and curbed by Gin acts of Parliament beginning in 1738, was beginning to decline. Alcohol abuse was one of the primary causes for crime in London, evident when the Salvation Army began its mission. Even children, as young as twelve, reported as alcoholic.[16]

This pattern and frequency of religious work was on the rise, not just in Great Britain, but eastern countries as well. The Baha'i World Faith came on the scene in 1863. A matter of coincidence, just two years before William Booth began the Salvation Army. The founder of the Baha'i Faith, Baha'u'llah, born in Persia, November 12, 1817, and at twenty-seven, set out to capture the world for Islam.

Capturing the imagination of race, culture, class, and nations as a whole, it spread its teaching of faith by works through planet earth. The difference between; the Salvation Army is an instrument of Yahweh reaching out to the world for Christ. The Baha'i, is an instrument for Allah reaching out to the world for Baha'u'llah. Both focus on the children, youth, social gatherings, and religious study. This attribute of faith shows frequency in a pattern of extremities involved with a doctrine of works and reaching out to those in community.

The Salvation Army, not widely known as a church, declined to administer the sacraments of Baptism and Communion. The sacraments speak to, and commemorate the life, death, and resurrection of Jesus. They believe, Christians who come to rely on outward signs of grace, lose the deeper meaning of Grace. Membership requires total abstinence of alcohol, drugs, and gambling, and in so doing, ask adherents to sign a pledge of allegiance. On the other hand, the Baha'i deny the supremacy of God, man's fall from grace, and teach the pursuit of education in meeting the need of humanity.

The Salvation Army grew rapidly. It did however generate some opposition. In particular, pubs were complaining of losing business because of opposition to their use of alcohol. Salvationists, now prohibited from entering public taverns and holding street meetings, lost their right to evangelistic public meetings. Some were met with stone throwing, public beatings, for sharing the War Cry, an international magazine of the Salvation Army. This pattern of persecution, expected, but did not deter their compassionate outreach for the lost.

The Salvation Army, similar to the pattern of the Methodist Church, holds the meaning and method of prayer sacred. Branded by the methodical way they order their lives, Major Carol Wilkins and Linda Faye Jones, USA Central Territorial Headquarters fell under an eastern and cultic methodology.[16] They put forth the concept of a Prayer Labyrinth. This model, used as a model for prayer and enlightenment would provide a deeper meaning of Grace. Unfortunately, the many years serving as Salvation Army Officers did not deter them from a system of symbolism, idolatry, and collective worship as related to eastern mysticism. Those reading this book and knowing the officers in question, please have compassion, love them as brethren, and be courteous. (1 Peter 3:8)

Similar in frequency, the pattern of convening circles seen in the Baha'i study circle, teach daily prayer and fasting as a form of learning how to systematize education as a spiritual concept. Study circles shy from formally taught classes, but led by a tutor, their role it is to facilitate the rhythm, and pace of the circle of study. Wherein attendees, participate in patterns of process, and facilitate learning. [17]

The prayer labyrinth, as understood, is a design for people desiring to have personal time with their god of reason, a pagan practice. Their desire to understand who they really are, and gain a closer walk with Jesus. In contrast, the nine prayer stations is similar to frequency and pattern of nine manifestations of the Baha'i World Faith. The numeral nine is a religious symbol. Taken from Arabic term Baha'i, it means splendor, glory, and link to a symbolic nine-pointed star. The phase, "Ya Bahaullah", Baha'i World Faith pattern of prayer and declaring, "O Glory of the Most Glorious." [17]

Please, do not think for a moment, that if Majors Wilkins and Jones knew the connection to the Baha'i, they would not have proposed the prayer labyrinth to Salvationists. Each station of the prayer labyrinth is similar to the teaching of Bahaullah. He believes in one God, as metaphysical monism, one who has no equal. The Devil also believes in one God.

The Holy Trinity of the Christian belief is contradictory, and the attributes of God, unknowable.[6] The Majors needed, as do others who stray from traditional theology, to search the scriptures for in them think they have eternal life, and testify they are of Christ. (John 5:39)

So far, this chapter shows a parallel. Frequency, shown as a pattern of behavior, enhances religious determination. The Salvation Army Movement, and its counterpart, the Baha'i World Faith Movement demonstrate the danger in bringing together patterns and frequency of mysticism as a model demonstrating the benefits of prayer. Employed in aboriginal settings, the medicine wheel; a Native American ceremonial tool and sacred circle, demonstrates the benefits of prayer.

What is the focus of Religious Movements? Is it not to show how to enhance the frequency and pattern of a spiritual experience? Not all have an experience similar to Paul on the Damascus road. His encounter with the Lord Jesus brought about blindness, subsequent healing and ministry as teacher of Gentiles. However, modifying traditional means of grace, through prayer and meditation, affects salvation.

Salvationists would be the first to object, and to affirm their prayer walk focuses on Jesus Christ, is not a pagan practice. That may be true, but it does not excuse the fact that the labyrinth, by very nature, is inter-religious, deeply mystical, and found in many a pagan practice.

If the Salvation Army expects God to bless their prayer labyrinth experience, then how does the Salvationist explain the scriptural passage, "Be not unequally yoked together with unbelievers: what fellowship has righteousness with unrighteousness; what communion has light with darkness?" These Salvation Army officers overlooked for some reason, the caution given of Paul. As a Salvationist since 1985, the author believes the Christian to be the temple of the living God; as God said, "I will dwell in them, and walk in them; and I will be their God, and they shall be my people." It is regretful to chastise two officers of the Salvation Army, but their pattern and frequency of paganism as a prayer model, is unacceptable, and must stop now! (2 Cor. 6:14-16)

With all due consideration, with comment, and explained in brief, this is how the prayer labyrinth works. [15] The prayer labyrinth, designed for a searching Christian, to find peace with God. Understand the affinity, having things in common, and interpret the possibility some activities should or should not go together with Christ. A Christian, raised together with Christ, sits at the right hand of God in Christ, need no prayer model to enhance the prayer experience. (Eph. 2:6) However, should Christian pass through these nine stations, must agree to have prayer journal in hand, herein lay some caution. Upon entering, sense the atmosphere of the room. Observe the low lighting, listen to the worship and music of praise hovering throughout the room. Notice the exotic table clothes combined with inspirational scripture, art, the cross, flowers, all set the atmosphere for prayer.

Your first stop suggests you: Bless your enemies and forgive others. Jesus said, "Love your enemies, bless them that curse you, do good to them that hate you, and pray for them which despitefully use you, and persecute you." All well and good, but then what are these small stones, are they not representative of an alter, a basin to wash, a towel and trashcan to clean up the mess of a sacrificial lamb? They appear similar to elements that might be found in the Holy of Holies descried in the Old Testament. Yes, Christian as a Holy Priest, but is this an appropriate setting for 2013?

As a priest, meditate upon these things. Give yourself wholly to them justify the appearance of prayer. Ponder on those people you consider enemies, and when a name comes to mind, pick a stone and print the person's initials. Hold the stone in your hand, and say a "prayer of blessing" for that person. Wash the stone in water. Allow God to wash away the bad you have against that person, even as the water washes off the initials. Wow to assimilate the washing of blood as washing a stone is this not heresy? As living stones, a built up spiritual house, we as a holy priesthood, offer spiritual sacrifices, not small river stones. (1 Peter 2:5)

The second stop along the way. Light a candle of hope. Take note the lights are without flame. You would not want to burn the flat map of the world, brought in for reference. Now, just believe in the hope that charges through tragedy and brokenness of life. Take up and light the candle. The candle symbolizes an offering of prayer to God. Share hope with God, and watch the smoke of the candle, prayer rising up to God.

What is this? What happened to our walk in love? Was it not that Christ loved us, and gave Himself as an offering and sacrifice to God, a sweet smelling savor. Is this not better than reverting to lighting a candle? God prepared Jesus, a body as a one-time offering, for our salvation. This offering must be an abomination to God. Jesus said, You are they which justify yourselves before men; but God knows your heart for that which is esteemed among men is abomination in the sight of God. (Luke 16:15; Eph. 5:2)

The third step along the way; To be like Christ. We talked about wanting to be like Christ earlier. Here we have the prayer labyrinth telling us its okay to want to be like Christ, a god! When we choose to follow Christ, we give up control of our life and become Christ-like in character. God intended we be honest, loving, humble, patient, kind, merciful and full of grace, but this is the work of the Holy Spirit. Just like Christ! These attributes already belong to Christian, but in the labyrinth walk, become as little gods.

This step completely loses sight of the scripture reference. Christ is asking us to follow Him in death, not to control life. The fruit of the Spirit is love, joy, peace, longsuffering, gentleness, goodness, faith, meekness, temperance: against such there is no law. They that are Christ's have crucified the flesh with the affections and lusts. So, if we live in the Spirit, let us also walk in the Spirit. Again, we are not little gods. This is new age teaching. (Luke 9:23; Gal. 5:22-25)

Notice, the characteristics of Christ are on the table, not in the Christian. The power bars represent discipline. God fills you with strength and self-control. The bread represents honesty. The candy hearts represent love. The granola bars humility. The beef jerky represents patience. The wafers represent kindness. Chocolate represent grace. The food you are eating becomes a part of you. Imagine how the Holy Spirit will do the same. Each food becomes a part of you.

Food, matter and substance, become part of the body. Now that is pluralism, the theory that reality is made quantitatively of many things. A term used to describe the acceptance of all religious paths as equally valid, promoting coexistence, a New Age philosophy.

The next step is number 4 of 9, the fruit of the Spirit. Before you go, pick up some disposable cups, nine types of juice, nine pitchers, and napkins. Observe the table. There are nine pitchers of fruit juice. All labeled as fruits (plural) of the Spirit. Consider which one of nine lacks in your life. Pour some into a cup. Pray that God would fill with that fruit and let it grow. Then drink. The symbolism, of drinking from the cup, symbolizes openness to God changing and filling.

Think for a moment, Paul called it fruit. Some develop tiny buds, barely noticeable in life. Others open as beautiful, fragrant, and fragile blossoms. Those blossoms produce small, hard, unripe fruit that grows and develop to maturity.

Notice: start small, as a progressive thought pattern open your mind to familiar spirits, who then takes up residence. Scripture warns of deceiving spirits, false manifestations, and found among God's people in these latter days. False prophets, will rise and show great signs and wonders, where possible, even deceive the very elect. The Holy Spirit warns that in the latter days some will depart from the faith, giving heed to deceiving spirits and doctrines of demons.

Callously calling them fruits is in bad taste, but according to Paul, the phrase is fruit of the Spirit. The Holy Spirit does not consist of many fruits, but of one fruit consisting of love, joy, peace, patience, kindness, goodness, faithfulness, gentleness, self-control; against such things there is no law. (Mat. 24:24; 1 Tim. 4:1; Gal. 5:22)

The next step within the labyrinth, number five; The day of discovery.  Bring along a portable DVD player/computer with the sound of ocean waves rolling softly upon the shore, a bench area rug, and some sea glass pebbles. Now, pretend you are sitting lazily upon the beach, the area rug being the sand. While observing the scenery, listen to the waves of the ocean licking at your feet. Pick up a piece of sea glass from the beach and look at it. Is it not interesting that the water has eroded the edges of the glass? See yourself as a piece of sea glass. Realize the work God has done for your life. God began a great work in your life, will He not continue?

Step five provides a sense of awe and accomplishment, even to the point where you claim your own salvation. The Bible suggests that as having obeyed, not as in my presence only, but now much more in my absence, work out your salvation with fear and trembling. Here the instructions stop. They want you to believe you can work out your own salvation. They fail to mention, it is God who works in you both to do His will and to do of His good pleasure. (Phil. 2:12-13)

Step into number six; Be assured you are God's Image. You bring a framed mirror, some post-it notes, and pencils. Open with a scripture reading, "Then God said, "Let us make man in our image, according to our likeness." (Genesis 1:26) Take a reading of your pulse caused by your heart pumping the blood through your veins. What you feel is life; A gift from God your maker! Now look in the mirror. What do you see? A body? A soul? A mind?

When you see your image do you cringe or praise God? Look closely, ask God to show you the real you. Then, take a post-it note and write a short prayer. Place the note on the mirror's frame. Some short examples: "May others see Christ in me;" "Use me to love others;" "Help me to love as Jesus loved."

Not such a bad scenario, except it is missing the spirit. Why is it, that modern day scholars cannot get past the fact that Christian is tripartite, a three part being consisting of body, soul, and Holy Spirit. The new creature, raised together with Christ, is currently in heaven. We have the mind of Christ. (1 Cor. 2:16; Eph. 2:6; Col. 3:1-4)

The fact is people outside and inside the Body of Christ, can see the Spirit of Christ in most Christians. The spirit of Jesus is in the Christian, and observed. Many give testimony of being in the world giving testimony unto the Lord, but the truths is, we stand in Christ giving testimony unto the world.

They see Jesus even as John said, "Life was manifested, and we have seen it, and bear witness, and show that eternal life, which was with the Father, and now seen in us." Not verbalized, but seen as different from another. The soul is the personality consisting of emotion, intellect, and will.

What others see in the Christian is Christ. He, by His Spirit dwells as our spirit. Our old nature, crucified with Christ, dead and buried. This place of spirit, emptied at the cross, and reserved for the Spirit. Familiar spirits cannot dwell together with the Holy Spirit in your body, the temple of God.  However, a familiar spirit can influence your emotions, intellect, and will. It is from hence the imagination, unless fixed on the Mind of Christ, and through indwelling sin, tear you apart at the seams. Under this condition, take each thought captive and bring it in obedience to Christ. (Rom. 6:3-6; 1 Cor. 3:16; 2 Cor. 10: 4-6; 1 John 5:21; 1 John 1:2)

Step number seven; God in the World. Bring a large roll of white paper pen markers. While in the station observe a large sheet of paper on the table. Take time to think on the two questions written: What is God doing through me, and as part of the Body of Christ, in what way are you being Christ-like to others? Is there more you could be doing? And what are you going to do about it now?

Difficult questions all deserving of an answer. In fact, God works through the Christian. We are ambassadors to the world. In this role, God through the Holy Spirit calls upon men and women to follow Christ, be blameless, holy, and harmless, the sons of God in His sight and without rebuke, in the midst of a crooked and perverse nation, because among whom shine as lights in the world. (Phil. 2:15)

Step number eight: Footprints in the Sand. Bring paper, place it on the ground and trace an outline of a footprint. Read the poem, "Footprints in the Sand." Let the reality of the poem seep into your heart and mind. Take the traced footprint and write on it how God is "carrying" you. Place your footprint on the walkway. This is not a difficult step and shows no practice of pagan worship, except for the theme of the poem saturating the open mind.

The last step is formidable: Confession of Sand. Bring seven small buckets seven scoops, a wooden cross, and sandwich size bags. The concept of sin: Difficult to accept, and when trying to be good, areas of life remain against God's ideal.

It is hard to accept failure, but even harder to confess failures to God. However, that is what God asks of us. The Bible reads, "If we confess our sins, he is faithful and just and will forgive us our sins and purify (cleanse) us from all unrighteousness." (1 John 1:9)

The bags of sand show areas of sin, Greed, Selfishness, Laziness, Temper, Jealousy, Pride, Indulgence, and Lies. One can carry this burden of sand picked up along the way, or leave it at the Cross. Place your bag at the foot of the cross. This is a symbol of giving your sins over to God. His peace and forgiveness will come into your heart and mind. We are all on the path where we need to be. A labyrinth is a symbol relating to wholeness. It represents a journey to centre of life and back again. Labyrinths, used as a prayer tool, lead to, what is within. A labyrinth has but one path, passed over in a single event.

A labyrinth involves intuition, complete with a degree of creativity, and imagery. With a labyrinth, there is only one choice, to enter or not to enter. One needs a passive, receptive mind. The choice is whether or not to walk a spiritual path. To walk passively means the mind becomes a receptacle for sensory experience, but there is a condition.

Throughout the Bible, there are indicators that identify false prophets, false teachers, false signs, lying wonders, and everything connected with deception. A passive receptive mind, associated with being empty, is one such indicator. Emptiness is a most deceptive enemy of God's people. In the latter days Christians, filled with the Living Word of God, need discernment. Empty Christians are not able to discern false doctrine. Only those Christians filled with genuine fruit of the Holy Spirit will successfully discern the counterfeit.[27]

Every spirit that confesses Jesus Christ has come in the flesh is of God. Every spirit that does not confess Jesus Christ has come in the flesh is not of God. The word "confess" carries with it the meaning of agreement. What the Holy Spirit says and does will always "agree" with everything Jesus said and did in the flesh. Jesus, unless proven different, did not use a "labyrinth" as a tool for prayer. (1 John 4:2-3)

The Salvation Army is the church of the author. It hurts to see how it may be slipping to a universal understanding of new Age thought and practice. The intent of this chapter was to reveal a parallel between a Christian religious movement and non-Christian religious movement. The Salvation Army, and the Bahai World Faith, bent upon a field of good works.

*Our Father, who is in heaven, hallowed be your name. Your kingdom come your will be done on earth as it is in heaven. Give us this day our daily bread, and forgive us our debts, even as we forgive our debtors. Do not lead us into temptation, but deliver us from evil. Yours is the kingdom, and the power, and the glory, forever. Amen.* (Mat. 6:10-13; Luke 11:2 NKJ)

The next chapter, the abuse and distortion, follows through with thoughts on the labyrinth, and where leaders distort the Christian faith. How easy it is to err from the way of truth.

# CHAPTER FIVE

# Distortion:
# The Abuse of Faith

There is nothing worse than the distortion of facts, taking scripture out of context in the attempt to modify a truth. Changing sentence structure, not only changes the meaning, but distorts the truth. In many churches, the reality of a living faith, disguised to meet the contemporary mind, often a distortion of facts. The unjust judge, who gave in to the persistence of the widow, did so to get her out of his hair. Yet, encourages us not to give up. The statement, "When the Son of Man comes, shall He find faith on earth" validates the fact that men ought to walk by faith, pray, watch, and not give up. Distortion of faith dilutes the truth. (Luke 18:1-8)

Throughout this chapter, we will attempt to understand why He made the statement about finding faith. Suppose, should Christ come today, would He find saving faith? A limited number of professing Christians know little about saving faith. Very few are waiting, and less watching for His return. Few pastors preach that Christ is coming soon, let alone the dead raised together in Christ, and having put on a new suit of clothes, ready made in heaven. (Eph. 2:6. Col. 3:1-4)

This promise, ready made in heaven, exclusive to the Christian. Given to those who have trusted, those who have heard, those who have believed, and were sealed by the Holy Spirit of promise, anticipate a redeemed body, fit unto the praise and Glory of Christ Jesus. (1 Thes. 4:16, Eph. 1:13) We too, as spiritual creatures abiding in Christ Jesus, sit ready for the fulfillment of that promise; to be suited in an incorruptible, immortal, perfect, sinless body, made in heaven. This, in comparison with New Age teaching;

> *"The realization of this is needed today. Christ in God. God in Christ. Christ in you and Christ in me. This is what will bring into being that one religion which will be the religion of love, of peace on earth, of universal goodwill, of divine understanding, and of the deep recognition of God"* (Alice Bailey, From Bethlehem to Calvary, Chapter Two: The First Initiation, The Birth at Bethlehem.

Under the influence of powers that were against the Christ of the Bible they communicated to her a distortion of what the bible says. It is only the believer in the Gospel that can have Christ in them. The distortion stands.[32]

We, being alive in Christ, wait earnestly for physical death, or upon His imminent return in clouds of the air, whichever may come first. Christian, hear the Word of the Lord, in a moment, in the twinkling of an eye, when the last opportune moment for salvation is past, the trumpet shall sound, the dead raised incorruptible, and we who are alive receive our anticipated inheritance, an incorruptible, undefiled, never to experience death again, a perfect, sinless body reserved in heaven, until that day. (1 Cor. 5:17, 15:52, 1 Pet. 1:4)

Again: It is not surprising to see Baird Spalding saying nearly the same thing:

> *"We know the greatest of all teachers came to show more fully that the Christ in him and through whom he did his mighty works is the same Christ that lives in you, in me in all mankind; that by applying his teachings do all the works that he did and greater works"* (Baird Spalding, Teachings of the Masters of the Faith.)

Of this glorious anticipation, few are those who hold it dear to their heart. Many do not know they do not know, some know, but do nothing. Rather, they seek some other way to fulfill the Gospel of salvation, found only in Christ Jesus.

The report of June 23, 2008, by the Pew Forum Organization revealed fifty-seven percent of Evangelical Christians think there are many ways that lead to eternal life.[19] This is sad, and a distortion of Biblical truth. Jesus said, "I am the way the truth and the life, no man comes unto the Father except through me." Faith comes through hearing, and hearing of the Word of God, but if one does not hear, how can they believe, let alone believe the Gospel of Salvation? How then could Jesus find faith on planet earth? (John 14:6. Rom. 10:17)

The most distorted doctrine in the Evangelical Church today is the Doctrine on Grace. See thirty-six abused scriptures.[40] There is no faith, than the Faith of Christ more abused. Given as a measure of Grace, Faith is widely misunderstood. How can fifty-seven percent of Evangelical Christians think there are many ways that lead to Eternal Life? Do these have the Faith of Christ, or do they just believe in Christ?

This modern day controversy, once again, revolves around abusive use of the English language. In translation, there are two interpretive phrases. One refers to the "Possessive Phrase" and the other refers to the "Genitive Phrase." The possessive phrase is subjective while the genitive phrase is objective. In the preface of this book, works is that of a child putting faith in a chair. Putting faith in a chair is possessive.

In this case, faith by works is an attribute of the child. The chair is merely an object of that faith. Should the chair be of a living substance, it could exert sufficient power to navigate the child to the chair, but a chair has no power to navigate?

In each instance there is an overt action involving work. The possessive phrase defines the Faith of Christ as a complete and subjective source. The genitive phrase defines faith in Christ as temporal and objective process. Faith, if not a completed work of Christ, then is but a work in progress. A work in progress means salvation requires more work. Thus, Grace is nullified, and the Cross an unfortunate incident.

Some may say they have faith, while another may say they have works: The former receives the Faith of Christ without works while the other abuses the faith of Christ by works. The following shows an abuse of a progressive work of faith.

Previously we touched on Prayer Labyrinths, and as a member these past twenty-seven years of the Salvation Army, some have fallen away from the truth, and present to its members and adherents another way to God. They do not appear to know, it opens the door to pagan worship. In due consideration, unknowingly they go so far as to list the benefits put forth by a Harvard Medical School research team, presumed to be a group of unbelievers, who advocate this as a spiritual journey.[15]

The benefits of the Labyrinth, and validated by research at Harvard Medical School's Mind/Body Medical Institute, and laid out by Dr. Herbert Benson found that by focus, walking meditations are efficient for reducing anxiety. Elicited, by what Dr. Benson calls the relaxation response, the effect of meditation has health benefits, including that of lowering blood pressure, and rate of breathing. Also, found among the benefits, were less incidents of severe pain, insomnia, and even empowered fertility. Benson claimed that regular meditative practice lead to power of concentration, and control of one's life. Walking the labyrinth is among the simplest forms of meditation. Demonstrative benefits led hospitals, health care facilities, and spas to install labyrinths on their grounds.[15]

Researching articles for this book, many references were found on occult and cultic practice in distorting the truth. Walking the labyrinth path to fulfillment, in my opinion, is like being drunk with wine, requiring multiple trips. Even at the Mercy Seat of a Salvation Army Corps, many people come forward on an alter call to be fulfilled, only to leave that place of Mercy without experiencing Grace. Similarly, how often does one drink alcohol without finding fulfillment? The saying, "One drink is too many, and a thousand not enough" is true for most. However, there is no distortion of truth in the Holy Spirit. He is the essence of all mercy, all grace, all peace and all fulfillment. Getting drunk with alcoholic beverages is a progressive activity. Filled with the Spirit is restorative; a once in a lifetime experience: Grace that is sufficient today and forever. (Eph. 5:18)

Many religious symbols distort the truth. Symbolism, set apart as a divine language, is an external expression of an inward desire to experience union with the divine. Labyrinths, used as a way in seeking truth, represent perils to the soul showing different ways of finding salvation.

According to Pew Forum Report, there are many perilous ways to eternal life. Though one cannot be certain what use labyrinths serve, particularly when so many programs of renewal sweep through the Christian church. It is important that discernment play a searching role in understanding the reason why things happen. Often in a fearful manner, many share testimonies of occult practice.[18]

Testimonies, difficult to deny, such as this one by Fritjoff Capra, Ph.D., physicist and systems theorist, author of "The Tao of Physics" who testifies to his experience:

*"Five years ago, I had a beautiful experience . . . . I was by the ocean one late summer afternoon, watching the waves roll in and feeling the rhythm of my breathing, when I became aware of my whole environment as being engaged in a great cosmic dance. Being a physicist, I knew that the sand, rocks, water and air around me were made of vibrating molecules and atoms . . . but until that moment I had only experienced it through graphs, diagrams end mathematical theories. As I sat on that beach my former experiences came to life; I `saw' cascades of energy coming dawn from outer space, in*

*which particles were created and destroyed in rhythmic pulses; I `saw' the atoms of the elements and those of my body participating in this cosmic dance of energy; I felt its rhythm and I `heard' its sound, and at that moment I knew that this was the dance of Shiva, the Land of the Dancers worshipped by the Hindus.´*

From this experience came "The Tao of Physics." He focused on the oneness of all things: he got the message from his experience. This is new age occult experience that everything is united.[32]

Sadly, Christians flounder in doing biblical research. Some open the door inadvertently to some questionable influence, not knowing the source of their peril. In seeking relevancy, many become emotional and mysticism becomes central in the experience of finding fulfillment. It is of no surprise how many become drunk with revelations, yet are never filled.

Labyrinth walks and journeys of prayer, even embrace the statement, "Can we be sure what labyrinths really are, and for what are they used? Are they a conduit for the mystical?" Not knowing you do not know is a poor excuse for even the question. The Bible speaks of Christian knowing the Mind of the Lord, and knowing the wrath of God is against ungodliness, and having the Mind of Christ, yet have the audacity to distort the truth in unrighteousness. (Rom. 1:18; 1 Cor. 2:16)

The historical source of the labyrinth goes back to stories of Queen Pasiphaë. She had a perverse sexual desire for a sacrificial bull, and the performance of bestiality. The beast was a Minotaur, having a head of a bull and the body of a man and lived in a caged labyrinth. Each year, King Minos, her husband, demanded that on her behalf seven boys and seven girls be sacrificed to the Minotaur. However, one year, a hero named Theseus accompanied the children, and taking a ball of twine to show him the way back, unraveled the string as he went through each station of the labyrinth. Once inside the labyrinth, he followed through each station until reaching the center. Here, he fought the Minotaur, beating the creature to death, and became a mystical hero. Though unaccounted, notice how Theseus sounds like Jesus.[17]

This story is a metaphor of the Lord. Showing the source of the labyrinth, it reveals the peril of what lay at the centre. The focus is nothing less than the divine sacrifice of our Lord and Savior, Christ Jesus. Truly, this is not the way to show the significance of the sacrificial death and resurrection of Christ Jesus. All who participate in this metaphorical form of ritual take heed, for they come under the wrath of God.

Many labyrinths contain halls and chambers. Similar to the Salvation Army's stations, and correspond to the ancient (and modern) spiritual, and progressive labyrinth journey of the soul. With many twists and ninety-degree turns, the ultimate experience awaits at the central point. The struggle with the inner monster (Minotaur) provides final victory over the force of darkness and ignorance, and the journey back to wholeness, and light of day. Can you see how this is but a metaphor, an allegory of the cross of the Lord Jesus?

The light of day, a daystar, sure words of prophesy. Take heed of this light, so distorted, and hidden in such a dark place, yet until the day dawn, and the daystar emerge as Christian's life, faith is lost on planet earth. Enlightenment of heart is as the day breaks upon the horizon, so is the cradle of His Eternal Life, our life. (2 Pet. 1:19; Col. 3:4)

Was it right to seek judgment upon an adversary from that of an unjust Judge? Yet, by perseverance, our dear widow was delivered of adversity. Deliverance and victory is available to all, but never in the strength of the flesh. It is a fearful thing to fall into the hands of the living God, and to do so in His sight, perilous times are imminent. The labyrinth journey comes in the design of many perils. (Heb. 10:27-31)

Similar to a Buddist Mandala, the design and use of the labyrinth design found in Christian meditation is a distortion of truth. In cathedrals of Europe, as Solomon's maze, and to alchemists, the fountain of youth, the going in and coming out symbolic images of death and resurrection. These images, designed as concentric circles broken at given points, (stations) describe this tangled, perilous web leading to damnation. As a new way to the divine, images represent the human nature and focus on self, feelings, emotions, ideas, and fuzzy thoughts of the mind. These stand in the way of divine knowledge. Labyrinths take one to the very centre of the flesh. This hidden inner shrine of the Minotaur, a stronghold of perils, and occupied by mystery, is the shrine of human personality known as the imagination.

Figment, an entity of the imagination, is a sure lookout in a stronghold of feelings, emotions, ideas, and thoughts, and is an interpreter of the knowledge of God. A believer who makes war against the flesh, does not know the power of God. A Christian may walk in the flesh, but does not war after the flesh. Weapons of warfare are not labyrinths, but mighty Words of God. The human personality, having access to the knowledge of God, fails to give heed to that power, even to the distortion of truth that leads to a faith of feeling.

Faith is not a feeling, nor is it a figment of the imagination. Therefore, cast them down, bring them into captivity; cause them to be obedient to Christ. He is ready to avenge, He is ready to punish, and upon obedience to the faith of Christ, that measure of faith given upon salvation, activated. This knowledge is of the Holy Spirit: His guidance, direction, and sustaining power gives victory over any, and all figments of the imagination. Dreams, hallucinations, schizophrenia, split personalities, all do bow to the effective, sustaining power of the Word through that Faith, found only in Christ Jesus.

Never even imagine you have two natures that war against the other, but know the Holy Spirit. Commissioned under the Word of God, at war with the flesh, the mind, and figments of the imagination, the fear of God is wisdom. Figments of your imagination, are the enemy of the Spirit, and want to lead you in a way contrary to the knowledge of God, but rest assured, God did not give the Spirit of fear; but of Power, and of Love, and of a sound Mind, ready to fulfill all aspects of the Christian journey through faith. (Rom. 12:3; 2 Cor. 10:3; Heb. 10:3-6; Gal. 5:16-24; 2 Tim. 1:7)

Have you, someone you know, ever been asked, and entered, to be a member of some secret society? Labyrinths are the trappings that lead along a single path. These, as in earlier times, used as an initiation to the dance, imitate paths of the sun and planets. They appear as patterns, portrayed on floors of older Christian churches as the road map to Jerusalem. These maps, used as labyrinths for those who could not afford to make such a journey for real.

Labyrinths, used as spiritual tools for New Age mysticism, esotericism, and occultism, are rapidly gaining recognition. If the labyrinth is truly a path leading to one specific point, the Christian traveler expects to experience spiritual fulfillment, a place of divine illumination. The labyrinth is a form of transformation. Its nature knows no boundaries, crossing time and cultures with ease, serving as bridge to the divine.

Strange as it may seem, the labyrinth is a spiritual tool used for right brain recipients, found across many cultures. The maze, on the other hand, is a left-brain puzzle. Thus, the labyrinth, involves the right side of the brain only, helps to access our intuitiveness, and provides a portal to the fallen spirit. Labyrinths enhance, balance, and bring a sense of awe to the sacred; a place where one embraces cosmos unity, and awake evil forces that elevate consciousness.

Man is a trinity of spirit, soul, and body.[21] Likewise, the soul divided by three components, the mind, will, and intellect. The spirit of man is consistent of intuition, conscience, and communion. The body consists of flesh, bones, and blood. The triunity of man prepares the reader for what may be a distortion, and discernment provides the way of escape from the distortion of text.

Moving through a labyrinth changes the way of perception. It seems that the inner, outer, right brain, and left-brain, reorients through an organized series of paths, represented by a realm of gods and goddesses associated with planetary movement, that dance to the tune of the fallen spirit.

Illumination is the goal of esoteric philosophy; the central arena for the occult. A former paragraph would show this central area of the occult to be the human spirit. This is the place where the righteousness of God resides. Therefore, since there is room for only one spirit, wherein abides the Holy Spirit. It is obvious that the labyrinth walk is but of the human soul under the influence of a fallen spirit.

Is the labyrinth symbolic of man's search for truth? Occult scholars tell us that the labyrinth symbolizes, "The difficulty of finding the Path to God." For the Christian, there is one path to God. The occults have distorted the truth, for it is God searching the mind and consciousness of heart, He knows what is the mind of the Spirit, and makes intercession for the saints according to the will of Father God. (Rom. 8:27) Their distortion of truth points to the mystical realization of one's divinity. Man is a god in the making, and as in the mystical myths of Egypt, and molded on the potter's wheel. This light shines in preserving all things; it is unfolding of the inner Temple of man. Again, a distortion of truth, the born again Christian is the Temple of God, in which dwells the Holy Spirit of God.

This book speaks to the Christian. Therefore be assured, you are the Temple of God. The Spirit of God dwells in you. Any defilement found in this Temple, God destroys. The Temple of God is holy, and that place reserved for the Holy Spirit is now the nature of God. Emptied through the efficacy of the cross, we give allegiance to God the Holy Spirit.

There is no agreement in this Temple of God for idols? Reckon it as so we are the Temple of the living God. God said, "I will dwell in them, I will walk in them, I will be their God, and they will be my people." With this assurance of salvation, how should we then live? The Temple of the Universe, the Temple of the Earth and the Temple of Life are NOT the Temple of Man. This is why the time has come for discernment, a work of restoration. (1 Cor. 3:16, 17, 6:19; 2 Cor. 6:16; Gal. 2:20)

Part and parcel of labyrinth symbolism is the initiation: a process of inner transformation; another distortion of truth. Paul, in Romans 12:1, 2 said, "I beg you therefore, brethren by the mercies of God, present your bodies a living sacrifice, holy, acceptable unto God, which is your reasonable service. Be not conformed to this world: but be transformed by the renewing of your mind, that you prove what is that good, and acceptable, and perfect, will of God." Distorted beyond measure, this text is abused by many so-called Christian movements.

Paul urged the Christian, that upon salvation they present the body, this Temple of God, a living sacrifice to God. This dwelling place of the Holy Spirit, now holy, and acceptable unto God, is a reasonable request. Recall in Jerusalem, Jesus went into the Temple, and saw goods being sold and purchased, how He overturned tables, cast out the vendors, and those that sold doves. In fact, He would not even allow them to carry their chairs and tables through the temple. Therefore, do not present your body cluttered by the world. Reckon your mind, now transformed by the mind of Christ, as renewed. This intellectual component of the soul harness, what is that good, acceptable, and perfect, will of God. (Mark 11:15-16; Rom. 12:1-2; 1 Cor. 2:6)

Compare the King James with the New International Version of the Bible. *Therefore, I urge you, brothers and sisters, in view of God's mercy, offer your bodies as a living sacrifice, holy and pleasing to God—this is true and proper worship. Do not conform to patterns of this world, but be transformed by the renewing of your mind. Then you will be able to test and approve what God's will is — his good, pleasing and perfect will.* Is worship not a distortion of truth? We worship God in praise and thanksgiving, not in sacrifice. Christians need to understand that any interpretation must be made from the standpoint of whom they are in Christ, and in this case, the Temple of God, the place of sacrifice.

Esoteric societies and the occult employ initiation to process spiritual advancement. The Christian too, must go through the process of initiation. We are, according to the plan of Salvation, chosen before the foundations of the world to be holy and without blame before Him in Love. (Eph. 1:4) Compare, that of the labyrinth symbolism, with that of the salvation experience. In research, and blown away by much literature on occult practice, there are many references for Christians to research. There is no end of distortion, even in modern churches that appear blessed of God. It is for that purpose, the writing of this book. When Jesus returns for His Bride, the church, will He find the faith given as multiplied?

However, we must consider archetypes of the occult. Freemasonry: under the Masonic candidate initiation, one led throughout the Lodge room, is on an invisible path from station to station. Each path, a journey into exoteric experiences with meanings cloaked in allegory, symbolism, and understood only by the enlightened few inner circles of friends.

Upon completing the journey around the Lodge, the initiates stand in the center of the room. Here, they kneel before an altar of an unknown god. The Master asks of the candidate, "What is it that you most desire?" Their response is, 'Light'. This "light" is some spiritual illumination involving divine knowledge. Jesus Christ is the "Light" of Christianity. How distorted is light substituted by Satan, who reveals himself as an Angel of Light. It just seems so unreal!

Nevertheless, we understand the spiritual emphasis placed on labyrinth walks of the Salvation Army. It is the symbolic journey of illumination, completely spiritual in nature, but dependent on works. Testing one's own power and strength in defiance of God's explicit will; it is a distortion. The path to the center is an invisible, yet tangible path leading into mystical ways of distorted truth. In search of the Faith of Christ, in all respects, very doubtful.

However, taking part in this esoteric way of fulfillment, many churches endorse the labyrinth journey as a tool that expands spiritual experience. One particular facilitator of the Labyrinth writes, "We are currently in a period of labyrinth revival. Churches, retreat centers and Christian camps are placing these prayer tools inside and outside. Christians all over the world are installing labyrinths in their yards and gardens. Many use labyrinths as a tool for ministry, bringing portable versions to prisons, and conferences. This is unlike the traditional Christian practice of good old Gospel preaching, and let God do the work of fulfillment."

Even so, some say God is blessing the use of the labyrinth; many drawn closer to Jesus, experience healing and gain spiritual clarity as they practice prayer walking on the path. In dedicating a labyrinth, those in attendance form a circle on the pattern to extend the energy that is in their hearts and minds to hands that reach toward the labyrinth. Points of energy, taught are New Age practitioners, show seven.

Following this exercise, a meditative time of laying hands on the labyrinth, and calling forth images of loved ones who walk the labyrinth. After this imaging, an exercise of prayer, "We dedicate this labyrinth to spiritual awakening, and with hearts extended in all directions, we call. "Oh, Sacred Sustainer, Way of the Holy, Creator of Possible dreams, Supporter for change, Forgive, Release, Make Free, and with Honesty, Wisdom, Hope, and Joy in our hearts ... Thank you for this beautiful spiritual tool on which we stand, Amen."[17]

Christians, holding to the exclusiveness of Jesus Christ in John 14:6 says, "I am the way and the truth and the life. No one comes to the Father except through me;" a serious rift exist. The very nature and metaphysical history of the labyrinth in spiritual pluralism is inescapable. However, with ever-widening inclusiveness, esoteric expression of the Fatherhood of God should not come as a surprise.

In view of a one-world Government, a one-world religion is a necessity. In the labyrinth experience, each station relevant, each path right, and each religion cooperative. In America, the Native culture puts forth the Medicine Wheel, where Man is in and part of the Maze. The Celts, a Never Ending Circle. One day a mark placed on the hand or forehead of those who follow this path, will identify their ownership. This is not the mark of a Christian, but the mark of the anti-Christ, 666.

The labyrinth, when partitioned as three parts, emphasize a state of cleansing, a place of meditation, prayer, and union. As one exits the path from the center, and enters the last stage, a union with God takes place. This Higher Power, in which healing forces are at work in the world, consumes the mind. Each walk on the labyrinth implies empowerment, and during the walk, each soul called out as complete.

Christ, Buddha, Mohammed, and the Baha'i, called in name only, has little meaning. It is the recognition of "light" rather than the bearer of light, that becomes significant. A Masonic member has freedom to worship at any shrine, bowing before every altar, be it temple, mosque, church, or cathedral, the realization of the oneness of all, a spiritual truth, howbeit a distorted truth. The labyrinth, by its nature distorted by reason, is a mystical aid to fulfillment. These distortions of religious truth act upon many faiths. Out of each spiritual encounter, some clipping takes place. Yet, this eventually brings inclusiveness to the universality of one world faith, the basis for a new world civilization.

You may be asking, is God behind the religious movements? How can God build on something that has origins in esoteric doctrine and pagan mythology? Rest assured, it is not the God of Abraham, Isaac, and Jacob who stands behind these distorted truths. God has blinded their eyes, hardened their heart that they should not, for if they perceived, understood they would convert, and God could heal. Further to their case, the god of this world blinds the mind of the unbeliever to keep them from seeing the light of the glorious gospel of Christ, who is the image of God. (John 12:40; 2 Cor. 4:4)

Now you know the devil blinds the mind of unbelievers, and you know God blinds the eye, hardens the heart of believers. Compare the Old Testament, where God speaks of how Israel will find rest upon crossing Jordan with the New Testament, where He speaks to those who have crossed over and entered His rest. They, who have entered into His rest, cease from doing their own work, even as God rested, and ceased work on the seventh day. Therefore, we who once labored have now entered rest. A warning to those who fall back into the work of fulfillment: If you as a believer, and your mind being darkened, your knowledge of God is but a figment of imagination. (Deut. 12:1-14; Heb. 4:9-11)

Throughout this chapter, we attempted to understand more fully the prayer labyrinth, and its manner of distorting the truth. However, the underlying reason for employing such a tool, not documented other than the experience. Perhaps, jumping out of an airplane makes more sense. At least, one might die trying to fly. In keeping with the title and theme of the book, why Jesus made the statement about finding faith, let us add some wings, and look deeper into the human will.

What really lies at the centre of the labyrinth that so many Christians would follow such an activity? Jumping from a plane is one thing, and hopefully one does have a parachute. In order to do that, we need to search the scriptures, for it is in them, we find knowledge of eternal life: the Word that testifies of Jesus Christ, his way of fulfillment. (John 5:39)

On the Sabbath, a sheep market in Jerusalem near a pool having five porches, a prepared feast in honor of the Lord Jesus. Close by a number of persons, having debilitating diseases, blind, handicapped, paralyzed, and others waited for the water in the pool to bubble. It seems an angel, from time to time, went down into the pool, causing the water to bubble. Whosoever made it first to the water was healed.

Now one man, being handicapped some thirty-eight years, could not maneuver his way to the pool without help. When Jesus saw him, and knew he had been there a long time, said to him, "Would you like to be made well?" The man answered him, Sir, I have no man to put me into the pool when the water bubbles, but while I am preparing to come, another steps in front. Jesus said to him, "Rise, take your bed, and walk." Immediately the man, fulfilled, made well, took up his bed, and walked, and that on the Sabbath.

The Jews reminded him that was cured, "It is the Sabbath and unlawful that you carry your bed." He answered them, He that made me well, said, "Take up my bed, and walk." They asked him, "What man said, "Take up your bed, and walk?" He, that experienced healing, knew not who it was. There was a crowd of people and Jesus had left unnoticed.

Later, Jesus found him in the temple, and in passing said, "Behold, you are made well, sin no more, or a worse thing may happen." The man, leaving the presence of the Lord, told the Jews it was Jesus, who had made him well. The Jews then persecuted Jesus, sought to kill him, because of the work of healing on the Sabbath day. Jesus answered, "My Father has never ceased to work, and I too, cease not to work." Not only did Jesus break the Sabbath, but spoke of God being His Father. This made Him equal with Father God. With that, the Jews really wanted him dead.

In contemplation Jesus said, "Assuredly, I say to you; The Son can do nothing of himself, but observing what the Father does, so does the Son. Understand, the Father loves the Son, and shows him things that he does, and will show him even greater works than these, that you may marvel. So as the Father raises the dead, and restores them to life; even so the Son gives Eternal Life to whomsoever he wills."

"Further, the Father judges none, but commits all judgment to the Son. All men should honor the Son, even as they honor the Father. He that honors not the Son honors not the

Father who sent him. Most assuredly, I say unto you, He that hears my word, and believes on him that sent me, has everlasting life, and shall not come into condemnation; and has already passed from death unto life." So much for the purpose of the labyrinth to bring about fulfillment.

"Again, Jesus speaks, the hour is coming, and now is, when the dead shall hear the voice of the Son of God: and they that hear shall live. As the Father has life in himself; so has he given Eternal Life to the Son, and authority to execute judgment, because he is the Son of man. Do not be taken in surprise by this; The hour is coming, in which all that are in the graves shall hear his voice, and come forth; they that have done good, unto the resurrection of life; and they that have done evil, unto the resurrection of damnation."

Jesus continues, "I can do nothing of my self, but I hear, judge, and my judgment is just, because I seek not my will, but the will of the Father who sent me. If I should bear witness of myself, my witness would not be valid. However, there is one who has borne witness of me, and I know that the witness, which he gave of me, is true and valid."

"John, bore witness of the truth. He was a burning and a shining light: and you were willing, at least for a while, to rejoice in his light. As a man I have no credentials, but these things I say, that you are saved. I have greater witness than that of John: for the works which the Father has given me to finish, the same works, bear witness of me, that the Father did indeed send me. The Father himself, who has sent me, has borne witness of me, but you have neither heard his voice, nor seen his shape. His word does not abide in you, for whom he sent, you believe not." (John 5:30-47) Thus, the purpose of the prayer labyrinth disclosed useless in testimony of truth.

Christian, search the scriptures; for in them you think you have eternal life, they testify of Christ. Yet, you will not come to Him, that you might have eternal life. He expects no honor from men, but He knows who you are, and that you do not have the love of God in you. Jesus came in the Father's name, and under His authority, yet you refuse to believe Him. Even when another called Thesus, having killed the Minotaur came in his own name, under the authority of another King, you receive and approve. Yes, Jesus became sin for us that we be made the righteousness of God in Him.

How can you believe, which has honor of another, as the Thesus of the labyrinth, yet seek not the honor that comes from God, and those who testify of Him? Do not think of Him as the one to accuse you before the Father, because he who accuses you is Moses, one whom you trusted. Nevertheless, had you believed Moses of the Old Testament, you would have believed Jesus, as Moses wrote of Him, but with a shrug of the shoulder, if you believe not his writings, how shall ye believe the words of the living Christ? (John 5:1-47)

Take what you need from the above passage, but if you are one who trusts in a prayer labyrinth, be assured the one in the middle is a raging lunatic with the head of a bull and body of a man, a Minotaur. In the ninth station of the prayer labyrinth, the instruction is to bring a wooden cross. There you place your sins as plastic bags of sand upon the cross, and believe Him faithful and just to forgive you, and purify you from all unrighteousness. Think again! (1 John 1:9)

As many believe, a Christian is but a sinner saved by grace. You, in all probability believe you need to have your sins forgiven again, and again, and again. Take notice, a Christian is one born of incorruptible seed, the word of God, which lives and abides forever. Would the Seed of God Jesus, having died on the cross, delivered you from sin, lead you to confess sin again, over and over? The terms "saved by grace" distorted throughout by many.

Christian, a true follower of Christ is not just "a" Christian belonging to "some" denomination, but one in Christ Jesus. Go forward through kindergarten and learn the doctrines of Christ. As a complete, perfect, spiritual creature, you need not lay again the foundation of repentance and confession before the cross. Abandon these works of faith, and trust the faith of Christ Jesus. Beware teachings on purification, laying on of hands, resurrections of the dead, eternal judgment, punishment, signs, wonders, and if God permit, proceed to a mature, advanced form of learning the Word of God.

Let it be made clear, it is impossible to restore, that is, bring to repentance again those once enlightened. Again, having experienced the heavenly gift, and being in receipt of the Holy Spirit, it is impossible to leave behind those principles concerning the doctrines of Christ. Moving on to perfection, and not laying again the Grace and mercy of God, flee the foundation of repentance through works. Knowing that the Word of God remains the mighty power of hope in the world to come, embrace the vigor of God, and with the faith of the Lord Jesus Christ, move unto perfection. (Heb. 6:1-12)

Can any, deviating from faith, lose fulfillment? Absolutely, but it is impossible to deviate from the Faith of Christ. Since justification is by faith, the just shall live by faith, happens once upon God raising Christ from the dead, it is impossible to crucify again, the Son of God. This would bring contempt, shame, public disgrace, and lack of the righteousness of God. Soil, absorbing the rain that falls repeatedly, produces vegetation whose cultivation benefits those who partake of the blessing. However, should that same soil produce thorns and thistles, and worthless, should it not be burned? Spoken that-a-way, be convinced of better things to come. Salvation is in good company. God, not liable to forget, but in labor and love for His name's sake, ministers to the needs of the saint. His desire for each is that they show the same diligence and sincerity in realizing enjoyment, assurance, and the development and surety of hope even unto the end.

This, in order that we may be encouraged, become spiritual standards, imitator those whose faith of Christ is an absolute trust, confidence of power, wisdom, goodness, and through patient practice, endure waiting the inheritance of promise. (1 Peter 1:23)

In conclusion, take into consideration those things said, and do not be in league with the unbeliever. There is nothing in common with righteousness and wickedness. Alternatively, there is no fellowship between light and darkness, and no metaphor of Christ in the Minotaur? What does a believer have in common with an unbeliever, and what agreement is there between the temple of God, the Christian, and idols? (2 Cor. 6:14)

What is missing in this chapter is a statistical process determining the number of women compared to the number of men that enter these prayer labyrinths looking for fulfillment. Men and women disagree with religion, life style, culture, ethnicity, and even marriage. The next chapter called, Faith: The Ratio of Marriage to Abortion is an attempt at answering the question: Why do we then marry?

# CHAPTER SIX

# Marriage: Faith in Divorce and Abortion

Why, do we then marry? Statistics show the situation of divorce is ridiculous in the United States, Canada, Sweden, Israel, France, Greece, and Italy. Divorce Magazine reports:

United States, 49% of marriages end in divorce, only 52% will last 15 years: First marriages last less than eight years. In Canada, 45% of marriages end in divorce. Sweden, 64% of marriages end in divorce. France, 43% of marriages end in divorce. Israel, 26% of marriages end in divorce. Greece, 18% of marriages end in divorce, and in Italy, 12% end in divorce.[24]

In the twenty first century, is it politically correct to consider the relationship of marriage? Keeping in context, marriage is an arrangement between God, man, and woman. In keeping God's plan for humanity, we are to multiply, replenish the earth. How many is too many? The world's population is more than seven billion. The new world order, should it ever come into power, plans to diminish that number.

The Triune God, Father, Son, and Holy Spirit said, "Let us make man in our image, after our likeness, let them have dominion over the fish of the sea, the fowl of the air, cattle, and every creeping thing upon the earth." Man consists of a triunity of body, soul, and spirit.

Accordingly, God created man in His own image, and in that image, male and female. Adam and his wife Eve, mother of all living, lived in a place prepared of God in the eastern part of a garden, called Eden. She and Adam became the parents of humanity. God said, "Be fruitful, multiply, replenish the earth, subdue it, have dominion over the fish of the sea, the fowl of the air, and every living thing that moves on planet earth. This command, in obedience to God, Eve conceived a child of Adam; One in the image of God, and one in Adam's likeness and image. The first, unfortunately aborted in the Garden of Eden, The second, just outside gates of paradise. (Gen. 1:22 26-28; Gen. 3:20; Gen. 5:1-3)

In the marriage relationship, a man leaves his father and mother and joins with his wife. Through childbearing, they become one flesh, not of many. One flesh indicates children of one true relationship. In today's culture, we see children conceived and adopted by those of different flesh, and lifestyle. That is, men with men and women with women. Children carried within the same or a surrogate womb. In some cultures, to keep the population under control, if the child is of female gender, in all likelihood, there will be an abortion or abandonment.

Recently, attending a wedding, the mother of the groom had her picture taken together with four different husbands. A second son stood as the best man, and two daughters on the side of the espoused wife, each conceived of different men. A divorce, according to scripture, is only by cause of fornication, but today, it is in mutual agreement. This fine woman, at one time, confessed to be Christian. Her promise, she would never leave her faith. It would be interesting to determine to what faith she was so committed. Surely, it was not the Faith of Christ. Is she one, wherein Christ is patience, will find watching upon return to planet earth?

The image of God, moral consciousness, is no longer part of the human spirit. Not only did Adam fall from Grace, and lose the spiritual image of God from within his loins, but his wife could not extrude children without pain. Understand, before the fall from grace, Eve was pregnant with child. In obedience to God the Father, they were to multiply and re-plenish the earth, so naturally Eve conceived of child. Unfortunately, Adam as protector of Eve dropped his guard, and allowed Eve to come under the influence of a handsome prince, and power of the air, Satan. This creature, entered the garden unnoticed, and planted a vine bearing seedless fruit, the same tree God had forbade Adam and Eve from eating; The tree of the Knowledge of Good and Evil.

Recall: God said that all the trees were good for food, but warned not to eat of the fruit of one particular tree. This was not a tree, but a vine planted by Satan to deceive. Eve, who knowingly took and ate fruit off the tree (vine) of the Knowledge of Good and Evil, shared with Adam the fruit of the knowledge of Good and Evil. It was poison.[25] Eve did not know just how harmful the fruit was to her developing child. The child aborted, and God had it buried east of Eden in the garden prepared for Adam and Eve.

Imagine the bloody mess of an abortion. Adam and Eve covered themselves and hid among the trees of the garden. Upon judgment, God ushered Adam and Eve right out of the garden, and guarded the entrance by two Cherubim and a flaming sword. The tree of life, prepared to feed perfect and innocent humanity, forbidden. Thanks to God, those faithful in Christ Jesus called saints will eat of the tree of life in the midst of the paradise of God. (Eph. 1:1; Rev. 2:7)

The first Adam, became a living soul, and fell from grace: the last Adam, conceived as a Life giving spirit in the womb of Mary, called Jesus. This Jesus is the Christ, Savior of human-ity, born a priest after the order of Melchisedec. Jesus Christ whose faith, saves. Now, we know that all things work togeth-er for good to them that love God, to them called in purpose, foreknew, and did predestinate as being conformed to the image of his Son, that he might be the firstborn among many brethren. Moreover, whom he did predestinate, he called: and whom called, justified: and in whom justified, glorified. What a glorious position and hope for the Christian. (Gen. 1:28; 2:15, 24; 3:16 & 24; Rom. 8:28-30; 1 Cor. 15:45; Heb. 7:17)

Adam's tarnished sperm was no longer able to pass to human posterity, the image of God, but rather the image of the devil, an entity of sin. Jesus said, "You are of your father the devil, and the lusts of your father you will do. He, a murderer from the beginning, abides not in truth, as there is no truth in him." The Word of God states, "All have sinned, and come short of the glory of God." Humans, conceived and born as sinners lost on planet earth. (John 8:24; Rom. 3:23)

Have you wondered why the Holy Spirit came upon Mary and she conceived Jesus of Nazareth? Joseph's sperm, as in all human men, consists of the entity, sin. What then shall we say of sin? Paul, in his letter to the Romans:

"I had not known sin, but by the law, I had not known lust, except the law forbid me to covet and to envy one thing and another. If it had not been for the law, I would not have recognized guilt as the result of sin. It was sin therefore, worked in me concupiscence, the desire for personal intimacy.

I realize however, that without the law, sin is dead. I was alive once in the loins of Adam without the law, but then through the law, sin came alive and I died. The law, being ordained to bring life, to me, became death. Sin taking opportunity of the law, literally caused my death. The law is holy, to obey, just and good. Why then, would that which is good cause me to die? Sin, put forth as an adversary, put me under the penalty of death, which is good, because now I see sin as being exceedingly sinful.

Christian, we know the law is spiritual, but as humans, sold into slavery and under the control of sin. I know, that what I do is not my intention, for what I do, I do not care for, and do not understand my actions. I do that which is against my knowledge of God and moral character, but then, consenting unto the law that it is good, I am in agreement with sin. Now I know and understand, it is not I who does evil, but sin that dwells within my soul and personality." (Rom. 7:7-17)

The book, *The Knowledge of Good and Evil*, by Joshua Collins, researched the meaning and position of Hebrew characters. Understand Hebrew is a composition of numbers, as English, a composition of vowels and consonants. There are words and places that are similar in structure and sound, but have different meanings. To illustrate, the word 'there' refers to a place, but the word 'their' refers to persons.

In this book, Joshua Collins questioned the term 'pleasant' to the eye as compared to 'pleasant' to the sight. Since God made every tree as 'pleasant' to the sight and good for food, but the Tree of the Knowledge of Good and Evil was not so good for food. The Hebrew word for 'pleasant to the sight', as compared with 'pleasant to the eye' have different spellings and different meanings. The one tree made good for food the other tree desirable to make one wise. The Hebrew term, 'to make one wise' is the English counterpart, intelligent, but without vowels mean, 'to suffer abortion'.[25]

Throughout history, the cause of humanities fall from Grace, considered a sexual act is not true, nor is disobedience. The cause for the fall of man was an act of treason, betrayal of trust resulting in the spilling of blood, and that of an aborted child. Many readers are going to choke on that conclusion. In studying Collins work, the following review shows how it diminishes from any possibility of heresy:

> Joshua Collins commands good composition. He documents with Gematria, an assignment of numerical values suited to original Hebrew. He shows how the Sanhedrin altered the structural content of Genesis Chapter Two and Three limiting the narrative to curtail the obvious knowledge of Christ to cover their own errors. Viewed from a cultural standpoint Chapter Three

appears, as some have concluded, sexually obscene, and shows Christ a liar. Trust the accuracy of God's Word and read, "The Knowledge of Good and Evil."

Eve had envisioned death. In defining the fruit of the tree of the knowledge of Good and Evil, the text misappropriated the intent of the word to make one "wise" when in fact, it is to make one "intelligent." When written without vowels, to suffer "abortion." Collins shows Eve conceived in obedience to God, ate of the forbidden tree, and aborted her first child. The intent to make wise, is Satan's way in casting blindness upon those who would interpret Scripture.

This fact proves accurate in today's denominational world of Christianity. Theology experts interpret scripture according to a fixed mind-set. Similar, to various passages of scripture found in this book, some scriptural passages directed toward the interpreter's mind-set, fixed to carry the intent. Can it be that the Word of God is without error only in the original manuscripts? The only true method for interpretation, find comparable passages that validate intent and meaning.

Satan deceived Eve by providing an oral interpretation. "You shall not surely die, but be as God knowing good and evil." This way, being wholly aware of God's written law, shared a limited version of God's command. To make one wise bears out the intent and meaning, "to bereave of children" and illustrates death as opposing intelligence. The scholars lead us to believe Eve did want wisdom, but according to the terms of Gematria, she observed death, and that aborted.

Reading Joshua Collins book, *"The Knowledge of Good and Evil"* we debate that interpretation. Knowing that abortion brings death, how could Eve justify the slaying of her unborn child through intentional consumption? Young women of today, intentionally harm their unborn children by subjecting them to alcohol and nicotine knowing it may bring death or some other debilitating effect upon their child. It behooves one to say; that this situation brought the world into chaos, debauchery, and slavery. One should understand how the intentional harming of an infant is even worse when having knowledge of death. That form of intentional misery, known to all, opens the door to every known good and evil.

Joshua Collins research on Genesis Chapter Three required articulate composition. Who could have known the original Hebrew text could be proof read with numbers? Gematria, a numerical sum of letters and applied to the Hebrew text, can be proved accurate, or inaccurate by its numerical sum.

Many, who stand on the inerrancy of the Word of God, when translated to English, would be better informed through reading Collin's book. Collins claims he is not an adherent to the philosophy of numerology, but supports its relationship with Gematria, as defined by a numerical sum, can provide interpretive meaning and intent of Scripture. Again, those, who support the inerrancy of God's written Word, could enrich their knowledge by the reading of Joshua Collins.

Gematria, defined as a system of assigning numerical value to a word or phrase, supports the intent that words and phrases with identical numerical values bear a relationship one with the other. The tree of the Knowledge of Good and Evil has by reason, a common root system. Knowledge of the one who would do good comes from the same source as the one who would do evil. Misappropriation of the term to make one "wise" appeals to the one who would support to "bereave" of children. In other words, cause to abort.

Knowledge, as defined by acquisition of wisdom and applied to the oral law of the Sanhedrin, opposed the written law of the prophets. Jesus, brought before the courts under oral law not the written law, crucified. Assigning numerical value brings out relationship as part of a "what for" in Judgment. Under numerous situations, Jesus referred to the written Law. Subsequently, not knowing oral law of the Sanhedrin, most laypersons do not determine the "what for" in bringing our Lord under judgment, and therefore misappropriate.

Joshua Collins brings out the term abortion, early in his writing. This was to show discrepancies in Christian thought and practice. He speaks of those who philosophize with disconnected and poorly quoted portions of Scripture. Upon coming back to the fact, he shows that the New Testament writers had little knowledge of the original Hebrew tongue.

Having come under the regime of Rome, Hebrew became a vocabulary of the past. All of this led to interpretation of the Scripture, and fragmentation of text leaving the church open to the acceptance of textual criticism. Using examples to prove his point, Joshua returns to the Gematria system of numbers to validate his hypotheses of the historical cover-up of the word "abortion" found written in the Bible.

Abortion, defined as a spontaneous expulsion of an embryo, or fetus before sufficiently developed to survive. Joshua Collins is clear in his deliberation of the process of abortion. He acknowledges, that over a period of time the probability of Eve having conceived under the influence of the fruit of the tree of the Knowledge of

Good and Evil, possible. This, in accordance to Collins, denied before Cain and Able appeared on the scene, and forever lost in interpretation.

According to scripture, Jesus was the firstborn of Mary, and as a baby, dressed in swaddling clothes better known as burial clothes. Jesus, in His immortality, brought to pass the saying, "Death is swallowed up in victory." Christ came as the second Adam, as well as Eve's firstborn, the son of Man.

So, when this corruptible shall have put on incorruption, and this mortal shall have put on immortality, then shall be brought to pass the saying that is written, "Death is swallowed up in victory." This assigned to the death of Christ on the cross, applies to all those who are crucified, buried, resurrected, ascend in Christ. Adam and Eve commanded to multiply, and they did, but when under the influence of the fruit of the tree, a derivative of alcohol, caused an abortion. Christ then, being accounted as the first born of the dead, lives as the eternal son of man, and begotten of God. (1 Cor. 15:54, 15:54; Col. 1:18; Rev. 1:5; Job 18:13)

The idea of a "Lock Step" formation presents the Garden of Eden story Genesis Chapter Three as being the fundamental building block on which all the remaining Scriptures are constructed. Suffice it to say, we are not meant to know the details of all scripture, but the Word of God. As guardian of the Way Jesus is all sufficient. Original texts if not available, but intended to appear, lose original meaning. Edited text, looked upon as numeric sequences of a flawless nature, unfortunately lost to most critics of the Holy Writ. (John 1:1)

Any biblical manuscripts remaining are copies of the original. The Word of God not passed away nor in a state of erosion, risks an occasional hurdle. Page upon page described in detail are elements of the heavens as a perspective of astrology. We see one, Joshua Collins, prepared to hear the words that describe an ignorant, rebellious woman whose desire to be wise, but who in a foolish agreement, consents unto the whims of Satan who misquoted the commandment of God.

Humanity did not fall as the result of an arbitrary piece of fruit from a forbidden vine, but humanity fell because the fruit of Eve's womb "faulted" by an untimely birth. Aborted, while thinking she was following God's will in replenishing the earth, the first-born child of innocence, "still" born. This is a collected transmission of eroded tradition that allowed Satan to fashion blindness upon all interpreters of scripture.

So, in today's denominational world of Christianity, how then can we find the Way, the Truth, and the Life? Instilled in the mind of Christian, the Word of God, and inscribed upon the very heart of the believer, the original text. Satan deceived Eve by providing an oral use of God's law. Understood to be the Word of God as written, proved to be a limited version of God's Word. To that end, Collins describes the intent of the righteousness of God. It is for our sake, God made Christ to be sin for us, who knew no sin; that we might be made the righteousness of God in Him. (2 Cor. 5:21)

Christ became one with the tree upon which He hung. As a wild vine must cling to a host tree to gain light and bear fruit, so the King of Kings must cling, as a wild vine to the cross to bring about fruit through His death. Joshua goes on to say that this was the reason why He drank fruit of the vine before His passing, and that purged with Hyssop, the fruit of the tree brought about an untimely death. This bears out in prophesy, why there was no need to break His bones. (John 19:36)

Collins, once again, brings the reader back to the tree of the knowledge of good and evil. Eve looked upon the tree as one to make wise, not as one good for life, described as the tree of life. The words, "to make one wise" misappropriated. The Gematria formula appropriate to the text, "to bereave of children" illustrates death. In this context, Eve did not see life, but the acknowledgment of death. Brought to mind by the Word of God who said, "But of the tree of the knowledge of good and evil, you shall not eat of it: for in the day that you eat thereof you shall surely die." (Gen. 2:17)

God said that the day you eat of the tree of the Knowledge of Good and Evil, you shall die. Now we know Adam and Eve did not die, so who did. Dare we suggest it was the death of Eve's unborn child was Adam's posterity? That suggestion would validate Joshua Collins work, "to bereave of children." (Gen. 2:17; Proverbs 2:13-18)

In full knowledge of the result, Adam and Eve partook of the forbidden fruit. Satan, in his subtlety, deceived the woman that this knowledge of death would not come upon her first- born, yet committed the first murder, and brought about the fall of man. Sticks and stones can break your bones, but words can never hurt you, now proven a false statement. Words can be for good or evil. Not only sticks and stones can break our bones, but words too, used to break and destroy the Word of God. How great it is, to be born again of such an incorruptible seed, the devil cannot touch. (1 John 5:18)

Having read the review, has it affected your thoughts on the Faith of Christ? Did it affect your thoughts about Marriage, Divorce, and Abortion? Do you think Christians understand how faith, knowing how humanity fell, would better manage the marriage relationship, and to refrain from abortion?

Statistics Canada no longer collects numbers on marriage and divorce rates, a sign of changing relationships. The agency published its last figures in 2008, the program on divorce initiated in 1972, and of marriage in 1921. The department of Justice maintains information on divorce, but no agency designated for marriage. In this age of more complexity and diverse family structures, the family as an economic unit is still a cornerstone of social and economic development.

With regard to abortion, scientific research from the World Health Organization in Geneva and the Guttmacher Institute in New York shows that outlawing abortion has not deterred women from seeking abortions. In countries where abortion is legal, researchers found that abortion was safe, whereas in countries where it is illegal, the procedure is dangerous. Globally, there are 28 abortions for every 1,000 women of childbearing age, and studies show that abortion accounts for 13% of women's deaths during pregnancy and childbirth.

The World Health Organization and the Guttmacher Institute released a study in January 2012, showing a global picture of abortion trends. The indicator, women are not influenced by the law in their decision to have an abortion. If illegal, women seek abortions in unsafe conditions and by untrained people. In 2008, the estimated annual number of deaths from unsafe abortion worldwide declined from 56,000 in 2003 to 47,000 in 2008. Complications from unsafe abortion accounted for an estimated 13% of all maternal deaths worldwide in both 2003 and 2008.[34]

Data suggests that the best way to reduce the abortion rates is to make contraception more available rather than banning the practice of abortions. The study found that in Eastern Europe, where contraception has become more accessible, abortion rates have decreased by 50%. The likelihood of a woman having an abortion is elevated if she lives in a developing region. In 2008, there were 29 abortions per 1,000 women aged 15–44 years in developing countries, compared with 24 in the developed world. Anti-abortionists suggest that the major reason women die in developing countries is not because abortion is illegal, but because hospitals and health care in general are lacking, which would not necessarily change if abortion legalized.[34]

Did marriage and abortion happen in Biblical personalities? Was Paul the Apostle married? The condition of marriage was mandatory for membership in the Sanhedrin. It seems Paul was married, but there is no mention of his wife, or having children. Unless Timothy, who his own son in the faith was his biological son.

Does it not seem strange that in three instances, Timothy characterized as being the son of Paul? Eunice referred to as mother and Lois as grandmother. Therefore, taken literally Eunice was related to Paul through marriage, and Lois his biological mother, leaving Timothy as Paul's biological son. Personally, why would that be so strange? The possibility seems quite rational. (1 Tim. 1:2 & 18, 6:20; 2 Tim. 1:2 & 5)

In the Old Testament, Judah had three sons, Er, Onan, and Shelah. God, because of disrespect, allowed both Er and Onan to die leaving Shelah, upon coming of age to wed their widow, Tamar, Judah's daughter-in-law. Eventually, Judah's wife also died, and after a period of mourning saw her as a lady in waiting. She realized that Shelah was grown up now, and she had not been given to him in marriage, so availed herself to Judah. He went in to her and she conceived twins. Judah, not knowing it was Tamar said, "She's not guilty. I am! She did this because I haven't given her my son Shelah to marry." Judah never made love to her again.

This story shows God does not favor the loss of seed. In the case of Er, he angered the Lord and he died. In the case of Onan, he let his seed go on the ground because he did not want to bring children under his brother's name, and died. In the case of Judah, until he knew the child was his, about to have Tamar killed, and abort the child. However, he repented and Tamah gave birth to a set of twins, Perez, meaning to burst forth, and Zerah, meaning sunrise.

Perez, according to the Gospel of Luke 3:33, is a descendent of Jesus. Perez, child of the widow Tamar conceived unknowingly of Judah who was the son of Jacob, son of Isaac, son of Abraham through Seth the son of Adam, the son of God. Think for a moment, if Judah had not been made aware of Tamar's relationship as daughter-in-law, but a one-night stand, there would be no Perez, and there would be no Jesus of Nazareth. It is evident that God intervenes in lives to bring about His intended purpose, in this case, the Savior of humanity.

This chapter related the issue of marriage, abortion, and extra-marital sex, and the Faith of Christ. There is little doubt as to the problems that give rise when abused. The one thing that stands out so clearly is the intervention of God in the lives of men and women of faith. The next chapter leads into the effects of faith in Christian practice.

In closing this chapter, is it heresy to interpret the Word of God using the model Gematria? Some suggest that the use of prepositions result in heresy. Many live out their lives in faith, but is it the Faith of Christ, or just plain faith in Christ? One applies to ownership, the other a gift of God. The next Chapter, the lack of faith should dispel any and all doubt.

# CHAPTER SEVEN

# Christian Practice:
# The Lack of Faith

Lack of faith in Christian practice, is an indictment of heresy, an accusation of doing something wrong, by experiencing something right. Some stranger walks into a church worship service, and listening to loud music, watching lewd dancing, crazy jumping up and down, laughing and periodic yelps, stunned. What are they thinking? These manifestations, not approved by the Word of God, show an indictment of heresy.

The intent of the next few pages is to show how the dance and other Christian practice, illustrate pagan ritual. Dancing, never an acceptable norm for Christian practice, yet in these latter days, taken over in sanctuary of the Christian church.

Many take the story of David dancing before the Lord as justification for dancing in the church. David, danced with all his might, wearing a linen ephod of gold, blue, purple, scarlet, and linen, designated for a priest. David prepared a new way of dressing and carrying the Ark of the Covenant, only to find one bearer of the ark, upon steadying the ark by placing his hand on the dressing, died a dismal death.

He decked the ark in the way of the Philistines in everything unacceptable to the Lord. God gave specific instructions for covering and conveying of the Ark of the Covenant to the point even touching would cause death. Uzzah, upon seeing an ox stumble, put forth his hand on the deck to steady the Ark, smitten of God. Now, that illustrates the significance of holiness. The journey stopped. The Ark placed on the side of the road in the house of Obed, for period of three months.

On the second attempt to bring the Ark unto the city, David danced again with all his might. Seems he had difficulty in hearing the voice of the Lord, or he was just not listening. A man thing! However, as the ark of the Lord approached the city of David, Michal, Saul's daughter and David's espoused wife, looked through her window, observed David leaping and dancing before the Lord, hated him in her heart. After the event, and the Ark of the Lord settled in the City, David returned home in anticipation of blessing his household.

Michal came out to meet David, and with indignation said, "How glorious was the king of Israel to day, who uncovered himself in the eyes of the handmaids, his servants, even as one vain fellow shamelessly showing his nakedness." David justified himself by saying, "It was for the Lord; He chose me above your father, before his house, and appointed me ruler over the people of the Lord, even Israel. Therefore, I continue to play this way before the Lord, and be even more disgusting, contemptible, mean-spirited before you in this, and insofar as the maidservants which you have spoken in concern, I shall accept their honor." Michal, though she loved him dearly, lived with him, but had no sexual union with him unto the day of her death. This story, used to introduce the chapter, "Lack of faith in Christian Practice." Where faith has no boundaries, excess of emotion is a sure indicator of the severity and abuse of faith. (Ex. 28:6; Num. 4:1-15; 1 Sam. 6:7-8, 18:6; 2 Sam. 6:6-23)

David's espoused wife Michal, hated his dancing, his music, and his rivalry. Inappropriate to the meaning of the Ephod a covering for the priest, this dressing was a loosely woven garment that while dancing opened the bearer to indecent exposure. Such is dancing in the church. Rhythmic body movements, the rise and fall of a woman's breast, and touching inappropriate parts of the body, inappropriate until very recent.

Now, it appears to be a way of expressing faith through praise and worship. What happened to the hymn, singing the words of a psalm, and spiritual song?

In earlier times, faith was of the heart, not of the emotions. The Charismatic movement began to play a significant role in Christian practice. Speaking in tongues, dancing, moving to sounds of stringed instruments, became an exciting change to the traditional style of church choirs, hymns, words of the psalms, and melodies singing from the heart. Faith became an expedient force appropriate to purpose.[26]

Faith movement supporters believe that faith works like a mighty force of appropriate demands. Through mere asking one can obtain anything, whether health, wealth, success, or what is desirable in the world. These are not of the Father, but of the world. However, because they lack the faith of Christ Jesus, seek what is appropriate to the desires of the flesh. Christians have lost the faith of Christ on planet earth. (1 John 2:16)

Through verbalizing and the repeated affirmation of words, selfish needs entertain the heart's desire. The formula is simple: "say it, do it, receive it, tell it. (1) "Say it." Positive or negative, act according to the expressed desire, you shall receive. (2) "Do it." According to the practice of your faith, receive it or at times you do not receive it.(3) "To Receive it." Simply plug into the endless storehouse of heaven. (4) "Tell it" so others may believe and receive your testimony. Jesus, alleged to have said, "If anybody, anywhere, will take these four steps, and put them into operation, he will receive whatever he wants from Me Jesus, or of my God, the Father."

As a former Charismatic/Word of Faith pastor, Ted Brooks wrote a book, *A Flaky Preacher*, (1999); he had an inside view of how Charismatic doctrine adversely affected the Christian's life. Ted Brooks came through the faith movement and entered the field of apologetics: The branch of theology that is concerned with defending and proving the truth found in traditional Christian doctrine and practice. Although the word 'flaky' is slang, but used extensively in church practice to describe Christians, preachers, leaders who do not remain established in solid doctrine and practice. Flakey preachers, filled with prophetic babbling, empty headed foolishness, and deep spiritual speculation, are in many cases, talented preachers who ventured beyond proper biblical practice.[27]

Some religious leaders are a threat to Christian women in church. It seems, according to scripture, they creep into homes and captivate silly, weak-natured and spiritually dwarfed women. These, often loaded down with sin and easily swayed, led away by evil desires, and seductive impulses. Behavioral patterns show many of these same women have dominant personalities that rule over husbands, the rightful position as head of the house.

Wives, be subject to your husbands. If they are not obeying the Word of the Lord, then through conversation, influence them unto obedience. Christians should model the marriage relationship in the bed and elsewhere. Husbands and wives serve each other mutually and in self-sacrifice. In years of biblical counsel, the position of husbands and wives, a point of rejection and divorce, (2 Tim. 3:6; Eph. 5:22; 1 Peter 3:1)

Understand Christ in relationship, as a significant doctrine. The desire to overrule often blinds biblical counsel. How do many Christian leaders show the appearance of accuracy of spiritual information when yielding to wrong spirits? How is it possible that false teachers deceive mature Christians, and some experienced leaders? Sadly, these counterfeit leaders have an effect on those who claim to have a mind of discern. The defense against false doctrine is to be well educated in the doctrine of Christ in relationship, but even then, how does one argue over emotional personal experience?

Not knowing the gift of God is the faith of Christ to believe, many lack true faith. Christian practice and experience, often lead to emotional chaos. Faith is illusive, but the idea that it comes and goes, not true. Salvation never leads one into a bi-polar experience. According to scripture Paul, when he spoke of faith, it was for clarity and purpose. It is not something wherein one Christian is exalted above another.

Accordingly, God dealt to every person, not many measures, but one measure of faith. There is Biblical evidence to show a measure is a filling, whereas measures like getting drunk. One is steady, while the other chaotic. There is a different meaning when foreign words are used in English. The article 'a' implies more than one, and the article 'the' relates to singular in quantity. The purpose of any increase in faith is not for boasting, but rather in keeping in touch with knowledge of the Son of God unto the measure and stature of the fullness of Christ Jesus. (Rom. 12:3; 2 Cor. 10:15; Eph. 4:13, 5:8)

There is no doubt that sensations can be overwhelming, but if one walk in feelings of the flesh, and not with knowledge of the Word, discernment between "personality" and "spirit" will not happen. Lack of faith in Christian practice, prevents the deeper reason for why things happen, indiscernible.

Even aware of the need for discernment, many pastors allow too much spiritual foolishness in church. It is not because they do not love the people; it is because they are afraid to confront them on their level of understanding. Lack of faith in Christian practice, hinders the proclamation of the gospel.

Have you noticed, that the appeal to repent, confess, and accept Jesus as Lord and Savior is lacking in the church? Even evangelical denominations fail to present an alter call. It is really, a matter of faith in practice. Jesus said to those Jews who followed, "If you abide in My word, you are my disciples, know the way, the truth, and the Life because the truth shall make you free." (John 14:6, 8:32)

Paul writes, "I fear, lest somehow, as the serpent deceived Eve by his craftiness, so your minds may be corrupted from the simplicity that is in Christ." Jesus came to be the one and only true source of salvation, healing, deliverance, and truth. God did not provide multiple paths to Himself. This seemingly narrow Gospel way is endowed by the power of God, more than sufficient for delivering the faith to practice. (John 8:31-32; 2 Cor. 11:3)

This Chapter is about lack of faith in Christian practice. In recent days a book titled, *Why Churches Die* by Hollis L Green, came to the attention of this author in 2008. Upon doing a review of its contents, it fits nicely into this chapter. So with some editing, adding and omission, it is under the Faith of Christ this review becomes part of this chapter on the Lack of faith in practice.

*Why Churches Die,* by Dr. Hollis L Green:

> Opening into a world of disrepair, Dr. Green takes the reader down a road of broken pavement. Where once there was a thriving community of Christian worshippers enjoying a Sabbath day of rest, and upon the first day of the week drink the Water of the Word. Refreshed, and being filled with the Holy Spirit, these worshippers are prepared to take on the following week, come what may on Monday morning.

> Unfortunately, that was yesterday, and no longer the case in today's worship. Many have taken the broken pavement as being part of a decaying, and disruptive landscape where Saturday and Sunday become the weekend of shopping, entertainment, leisure, and debauchery. The first of many, Dr. Green looks for the cause of broken pavement, and determines that a fault line runs directly under the church, whereby the church is but a place of refuge, rather than a sanctuary of peace and infilling. Monday morning comes into view, but with the glass half empty.

The great commission is as you go unto all nations teaching the good news of the gospel, and having believers baptized into the death of Christ. These are among the intents of worship, but now replaced with programs of entertainment. Dr. Green suggests the criteria for personal evangelism has changed from means, men, and methods to methods, men and means. This, he claims, the reverse order of New Testament evangelism. Putting the caboose in front of the engine is never the best order for moving goods and services.

This reversal of New Testament evangelism has closed the door to spirit filled ministry. Real evangelism, spontaneous zeal, personal enthusiasm, and a soul set ablaze by the Holy Spirit, lost on planet earth. The conversion experience and dialogue is perhaps the only real force for the advancement of the Faith of Christ in Christianity. However, complex methods and programming limit the mobilization of Christian movements. As the church becomes both the base and the field of operations, "go" now changed to "come" while the whole world perishes in the quagmire of troubled times.

Dr. Green emphasizes the problem of church growth may be partly due to the inversion of church priorities. Inviting the sinner to come to church that they be saved is not the best means of reaching the world. Inevitably, death comes upon a decaying organism, the triumphant Christ of the Gospel no longer prevails in church growth and evangelism.

Whatever else is the will of the people, the proclamation of the Gospel, downgraded to entertainment. The church now its purpose thwarted, has a growing gap in the pavement of despair as separating the pulpit and those in the pew. Dr. Green suggests, "cheap Grace produces poor worshipers."

There appears to be an inadequate comprehension of the conversion experience. This inadequacy is due to the lack of Christian discipleship. Christianity without discipleship, like a Christian without Christ. Christians are the living body of those called to be the faithful in Christ. These, sent out of the world are to be sent back into the world. Men form the precedent for standing in Christ, called to bear witness unto a dying world. It seems ironic, but Dr. Green implies that women form a supporting role in evangelism through prayer support, and reminds us that Deborah, called upon to Judge Israel, recruited Barak to go into battle while she remained alongside. Barak was the champion of the cause. (Judges 4:4-9)

Why has the Church not grown in proportion to population?  Is it because there is more concern with denominational doctrine and theological bias? Dr. Green points out how doctrine in the head does not necessarily perpetuate growth. By finding its way to the heart, and manifested through each member, growth happens. The power of personal experience is often the means whereby church life transformed. Converts become members, taught in word and doctrine, believe, and go forth preaching the good news of the Gospel.

Inevitably, the church comes to maturity, a *status quo*. The image of material stability deterred the furthering of growth and vitality. The church prepares for death. The gurgling of its breathing is heard throughout the community, and the proclamation of the Gospel, dispelled. Church leaders have fallen into a state of mediocrity. Lacking the Faith of Christ, spiritual life has bred complacency, and retards the natural vitality of the Christian. The message of the Word of God is stifled among current events, and sermons mixed with social and political jargon.

Society as a whole is lost to a local congregation as mega churches take their stand among the culture and standards of the people to whom they minister. Small urban churches become lost in the jungle of the high rise. It is necessary to prune personnel and programs to fit the community in which one serves, and that means we must get back to the basics and taste the fruit of fresh evangelism.

The mission of the church is growth. Multiply and replenish the church should be the mandate of each congregation. The dynamic quality of the Holy Spirit is as present today as it was in the day of the Apostles, wherein the Christian is to be both the saved and the saving influence upon the world. The great commission has never lost its sense of urgency, and should not be replaced by fun, food, and fellowship.

Dr. Green suggests that these priorities are an invitation to come to church for fulfillment, and to keep the constituency happy. The church family becomes a paternal organization and inhibits the potential growth of the individual, and a "no-harvest" theology grows among its membership.

The church is in decline because the focus, placed on fellowship rather than discipleship, fails. The plan, person-to-person evangelism, is simple. Growth will be inevitable because God is the instrument of conversion while man is the conveyance and means in influencing men to repent and turn to Him for deliverance from sin.

Many in community remain unsolicited, except by the cult. The doors are open, the call to worship proclaimed, but the people are not coming. Is it because soul winning has come to an abrupt stop, or because the churchmen have become passive? Active soul winning must remain the criteria of every aspect of the church. The call to come is inadequate. Go and get them from the highways and the byways is the mandate of the New Testament Church.

Dr. Green suggests there is an active spiritual drift within the congregation of which the church is unaware. The first and foremost indicator of this situation is shown when most programs and activities are led by the same person(s). This leaves no opportunity for others who, in all sense of no purpose, begin to drift from participants to spectators.

Should a church consider a change to its doctrines? In most situations, the answer would be no, but from time to time a new application may be fitting. A church cannot grow unless fed from within the congregation. If the church has lost its fervor for evangelism, it will surely suffer loss.

Personal Evangelism has always been an effective strategy for church growth. The pastor and church leadership must take the initiative. If not, the church will become vulnerable to all kinds of disease. There is nothing to overcome. Any, who confess they belong to Christ, but does not go without the wall and bear the reproach of Christ, counted suspect to being wall builders. Don't fence me in, is a song of the fifties appropriate for church growth and membership.

Speaking of building walls and writing songs, modern man had built the computer whereby substituted revelation and faith with computer reason and logic. Conversion, lost in a scientific dilemma of bits and bytes. The goal of evangelism should not be to build a better processing unit, but to reach out with the gospel and create apps fitting to the Christian.

The latter phase of Dr. Green's book, *Why Churches Die* based on the need for revival. To this phase, renewal is the word that addresses the need to revitalize. Revival imparts the truth of rebirthing, a returning to the basic laws of growth. Speaking to the need for leadership, unless the leader is the husbandman, and taste the first fruit of the harvest, he will not know how to train the reapers.

With an eye on the harvest, a husbandmen's responsibility is to care for the growing plant. Some picked at random others used for seed. However, evangelism intertwined with revival became synonymous. Whatever happened to soul winning? All delivered to the evangelist, the preacher of revival, and lost in the organization of institution. There is no faith.

What ever happened to the priesthood of the converted? Believers encounter the sinner in community. This is where they live. The idea is to make disciples in the church and place them in community. It is not a necessity to view the church from a success attribute, but from an attribute of constraint in moving out of a mega church to a small group of compassionate believers with a love and concern for the lost people of planet earth, wherein there is no faith.

All this is fine, but what happens to those who do take the stand and go out into the world? Will they be welcomed, or even encouraged by those who stay behind? Often, any attempt to renew the spiritual life of the church, met with animosity, and that from a legalistic institution that reached the paradigm of its success, and not to break the status quo.

No man, confessing Jesus Christ as Savior and Lord, would intentionally hinder God's scheme of redemption. Yet they do, and yes they have, and will continue to hinder the cause of Christ on planet earth. Will Christ find faith upon His return, it is doubtful, yet Christian must prevail to that day.

The plan of God, placed upon the heart of man to motivate them to secure another, has yet to secure the Kingdom. The essentials of worship on the first day of the week compared with the Sabbath day of renewal, contribute to unintentional hindrance to the Work of God. Along with that, Dr. Green reiterates all as said of thirty-five reasons why churches die.

These hindrances of man, unintentional or intentional, the church must prevail until Jesus comes to retrieve those in whom His faith stands as a bulwark of His bride, the church. His bride and each confessing Christian sits at his/her place in heavenly places dressed in a suit made in heaven fitting for the attire of the children of God. Amen!

Research on this topic could be expanded to many pages, but in the interest of continuity, this chapter comes to an end. However, it opened by condemning the practice of the dance. In all fairness to those who practice, it is not so much as the practice, but the lyrics and beat of the music. It is the understanding of the author, that if any tune, practiced in the minor key, it is not of the Lord and should not be used in praise and worship. Not knowing the difference, it is not fair to those who, in faith, enjoy praise and worship. Enjoy!

This chapter revealed the place of lack of faith in practice, and in particular the Faith of Christ in practice being lost on Planet Earth. The next and final chapter, Salvation: The Cost of Faith on Planet Earth.

# CHAPTER EIGHT

# Salvation: The Cost of Faith

A significant number of Bible texts were necessary in this chapter to bring about a healthy understanding of the Faith of Christ, and some repeated for the purpose of clarity. Along the way, the text of Luke 18:8 highlights the importance of the return of our Lord and Savior Christ Jesus, but not before serious signs occur on the horizon. Watch therefore; pray always, that you may be accounted worthy to escape all these things that shall come to pass, and when overcome, to stand before the Son of man, redeemed forever.

Remember, it is not your faith that saves, but the Faith of Christ delivered as a measure of Grace, a gift of God unto all the saints. Paul said, "I say, through the grace given unto me, to every person that is among you, not to think of himself more highly than he ought to think; but to think soberly, according as God has dealt to every man that measure of faith. For every Christian is a recipient of the grace according to the measure of the gift of Christ. (Luke 18:8, 21:34-36; Rom. 12:3; Eph. 4:7)

Recall, that in the beginning, while desiring fruit from the tree of the Knowledge of Good and Evil, our first earthly parents aborted their first-born child, and as a result, judgment fell upon humanity.[25] This, the first shedding of blood, brought about judgment upon humanity. The second shedding of blood, the Lord Jesus Christ, brought about redemption for humanity. Almost all things under law purged with blood; and without shedding of blood is no remission. Each of us as human beings are so judged, beginning with the first unto the last on planet earth. Today, we thank God for His only begotten Son, the last Adam Jesus, who is Savior and Lord. (1 Cor. 15:45; Heb. 9:22)

The perfect seed implanted in Eve was lost, but never forgotten. The seed of Adam imperfect yet made a living soul; short the Glory of His Life.[28] The seed of the Holy Spirit, conceived in Mary, brought forth the last Adam, Jesus, made a life giving spirit. We know now, why all things work together for good to them that love God, called unto perfection.

According to his purpose, His desire, even before laying the foundation of the world Christian, predestined to have the characteristics of His only begotten Son Jesus: Now revealed is the Glory of His Life, and having the image of the Father, perfect. Thus, the perfect seed, once planted in the womb of Eve and aborted, takes root in Mary bringing forth the Glory of His Life to abide as Jesus of Nazareth on planet earth.

Further to this glory, those called, he justified, born again as new creatures without sin. Christ, who is our life became sin for us, and we, made the righteousness of God in Christ, are without sin. Christ, once offered to bear the sins of many, along with those without sin, now look for him to appear the second time unto salvation. Accordingly, His divine power gives to the Christian all things relating to life and godliness. How could this be? Through the knowledge of him who called us, set us apart, redeemed as the glory of His Life; Christ our Savior, made our life, wisdom, righteousness, and redemption. (Mat. 5:48; Rom. 8:28-30; 1 Cor. 1:30; 15:45; 2 Cor. 5:17, 21; Col. 3:4; 2 Peter 1:3; Heb. 9:28)

The first chapter of Hebrews explains it this way: God, who at separate times and under different circumstance spoke to the fathers, through the prophets. In these last days, speaks to us through His Son, Christ Jesus. This is who, being heir of all things, made planet earth as it is today. Jesus, being the brightness of his glory, and the express image of his person, secures all things by the word of his power. This Lord Jesus, of whom God resurrected, presents us unto the Father, holy, without blame, pure, clean, and separate from sin, having finished the work, sat down on the right hand of the Majesty on high. (Gen. 1:3; Eph. 1:4. 2:6; Heb. 1:1-3)

Continuing on to Hebrews Chapter Eleven, we see how faith is the substance of things hoped for, the evidence of things not seen. We know, through the faith of Christ, the worlds framed by the word of God. Things seen were not made of things that appear. The Faith of Christ gives understanding of things that concern Planet Earth. The world is not eternal, nor is it a product of its own making, but God created all things by Jesus Christ. The world, framed out of nothing, but His will.[32] Not having power of itself, the 'will' is an action causing things to happen. By the significant Faith of Christ, we understand the worlds without scientific proof. (Eph. 3:9)

It was by faith Abel offered unto God a better sacrifice than Cain by which he retained his righteousness. It was through faith Enoch, and taken to heaven without passing through physical death. Why? He just pleased God. Therefore, we conclude that significant Faith of Christ as better than any of that summoned up by the vanity of mind on planet earth. We know, and rest upon that Faith of Christ, as pleasing to the Father of light. Faith outside the Faith of Christ is not pleasing to the Father. Faith without doubt, surety of Eternal Life in Christ, and being made the righteousness of God in Christ Jesus, we stand before God.    (2 Cor. 5:21; Col. 1:12)

Noah, through faith being warned of things not seen, moved with fear, prepared an ark and saved his family. In this saving out of water, condemned the world, and became heir to the righteousness of God by faith. Water baptism is a means by which Christians give public witness. Through baptism, emersion symbolic of death, lifted out of water symbolic of the resurrected life. In reality, baptism is positional, whereas God places us into the death of Christ and raises us by the same power He resurrected Christ.[21]

Abraham, called to go into a place which after, he would receive for an inheritance, obeyed. Not knowing where to go, or how to get there, looked for a city with foundations, whose builder and maker is God. His wife Sarah, by faith receiving strength to conceive delivered Isaac when past childbearing age. Abraham, as one good as dead, now his posterity counted as stars in the sky, sand of the sea, all through faith, the fulfilled promise of God to all believers.

Abraham, being put to the test, offered by faith his son Isaac. He had received the promises of a multitude of children through Isaac offered up his son. Concerning things to come, Abraham obedient to God's command, lifted a knife to sacrifice his son, Isaac. The incident blocked by a Ram caught in a thicket, used as a substitute, and paid the price of obedience.

That cost of obedience, endured by God the Father when His only begotten Son, lifted up in sacrifice becoming sin, turned away. There is no greater cost, than losing a child. Jesus, endured the cross, there was none other sacrifice available. The judgment of God equitable, just to all, and because of conscience God directed, and by commitment placed us in Christ Jesus. God, by this purchase, made His only begotten Son Jesus, our Wisdom, Righteousness, Sanctification, and Redemption. Jesus knew no sin, but made sin for us that we, made the righteousness of God in Christ. See the preposition "in" as it is not our righteousness, but that of God who made Jesus to be our righteousness. Read this paragraph over, and over again. Grasp that full meaning of God's redeeming Grace, and though the Faith of Jesus Christ: The just shall live by faith. (Rom. 3:3-6; 1 Cor. 1:30; 2 Cor. 5:21; Gal. 2:16)

Moses was hid three months by his parents, because they knew he was a proper child and were not afraid of the king's commandment to have all the first-born children of Israel killed. Moses, also in later years did not fear the wrath of the king, and refused to be called the son of Pharaoh's daughter, forsook Egypt. Yet, seeing Him who is invisible, endured the cost of rejection. In faith, he kept the Passover, the sprinkling of blood on the doorposts, and in assurance that he that destroyed the firstborn of Egypt should not touch the children of Israel. Through faith, he led Israel through the Red Sea as by dry land. The Egyptians, deceived by sight, drowned in the water. Christ, who is the image of the invisible God, and first-born of every creature, was by faith seen by Moses. (Heb. 11:1-30; Col. 1:15; 1 Tim. 1:7)

Through Faith Moses, saw Christ in the fiery image of the bush not yet burned by fire. Herein, the righteousness of God revealed from faith to faith, and written: The just shall live by faith. The wrath of God, revealed from heaven against all ungodliness and unrighteous, cost Pharaoh's men and all their beasts, their life. They died without faith or mercy.

God revealed the invisible things of Christ from the creation of the world. Understood by things made visible, the eternal power of the Godhead, made clear to men. With regard to righteousness of God, they are without excuse. Even we, the twenty-first century Christian now see the pre-eminent Glory of Christ Jesus, the first-born of all creation, as the aborted child of Eve, the mother of all living.[25] (Gen. 2:15; Rom. 1:17-20; Col. 1:15)

What then, is the righteousness of God? Things visible are in contrast to things invisible, whereas righteousness consists of things visible. Christ, being the very image of God, made visible to the apostles through faith. In time, two thousand years ago, God placed us in Christ. The righteousness of God gives us the faith of Christ in which to believe that truth.

The cause of the resurrection now just, affected the means by which God made Christ to be our wisdom, righteousness, sanctification, and redemption. We know that an individual is not justified by works, but by the faith of Jesus Christ. We believe, justification is of the faith of Christ. Those who trust in the works of the law remain under the curse of the law. It is written, "Cursed is every one that continues not in things which are written in the book of the law to do them." Except the just live by faith, there is no righteousness, but all is lost on planet earth. This answers the question, "Will Christ find faith" when He returns to planet earth? What do you think?

God made Christ to be sin, who knew no sin, that we might be made the righteousness of God in Him. In Christ, we are the righteousness of God. It is through the efficacy of God that we are in Christ Jesus, and Christ, through the efficacy of God, made unto us wisdom, righteousness, sanctification, and redemption. ((Rom. 3:3; 1 Cor. 1:30; 2 Cor. 5:21; Gal. 2:16, 3:10; Phil. 3:9)

Righteousness is the putting on of Christ. A garment is the putting on of clothes. In putting on Christ, we are in a sphere of righteousness. However, by chance, if one claims their faith as righteousness, Christ died in vain. If Christ never rose from the dead, the faith of Christ would be dead, and we are yet in sin. The foundation of Christianity is the Faith of Christ.

Now, after putting on, entering the sphere of righteousness, there is no room for flesh. God, having placed us in Christ, made Him our Wisdom, righteousness, sanctification, and redemption. Christ, who suffered once for all, and all for sin, through death brought us unto God, and of His Spirit, abides immortal in our mortality. We, being born again as new creatures, rose together in Christ to heavenly places. Thus, we abide together in Christ. (Rom. 6:3-6; 13:14; 1 Cor. 15:14-17; Gal. 3:26-28; Eph. 2:6; 1 Peter 3 :18)

Now then, we have a discerning question, "How Should We Then Live?"[9] Should it be through faith, or should it be by sight? Through faith the Red Sea parted and the children of Israel passed over the Red Sea on dry land. On the other hand, Pharaoh by sight going in after with his chariots and horsemen, was swallowed up by the sea. Again, when the priests who carried the Ark of the Covenant came abreast of the river Jordan, through faith the soles of their feet lifted up as unto dry land. This marks the difference between the forces of good and forces of evil. Those who live by sight, count as loss, but those who by the faith of Christ, count as gain. (Exodus 15:19; Josh. 4:18)

We touched briefly on the fallen spirits (Angels) of the devil. By sight, these too can work miracles. Going forth unto leaders of the earth and to the whole world, they gather for the battle of that great day of God Almighty. Behold, the Lord comes as a thief in the night. Blessed are those who watch, and not found naked. Through the faith of Christ, and wearing the breastplate of righteousness of Christ, at rest. The seventh angel, having poured out the last vial of the wrath of God on planet earth, comes a voice from out of the temple of heaven, from the throne of God, saying, "It is done." (Rev. 16:14-17)

There is a character of a television program, 'Laugh In' at the end of the program exclaims, "It is over!" Yes, the day is upon all humanity, and many predict the end of this present age. This chapter, titled Salvation: The cost of Faith, written that you might understand the deeper reason why there are wars, rumors of war, earthquakes, climate change, and pestilence. These things must happen before that great and mighty day of the Lord. Now, let's go back to the beginning to review that which has been written, and necessary for recall. This is for reinforcement of truth.

*"God's way of working reveals His values in the same way as a person working reveals values."*

# CHAPTER NINE

# Conclusion:
# The Judgment of God

It was through Adam that death came upon all flesh. They, who receive grace, and the righteousness of Christ, shall be as one flesh. Therefore, by the offence of Adam judgment came upon all men. Their loss of life led to condemnation; but by the righteousness of Christ, a free-gift came upon all unto justification of life. So, sin brings forth death, even so, grace brings forth righteousness unto eternal life in Jesus Christ. Do not think that it is of anything you have done that God deals with the unbelieving, for God casts them out, not because of His righteousness, but of their unrighteousness. (Rom. 5:17-21; Deut. 9:4)

The righteousness of God, without law, is obvious to those who testify for the law. As said before, the righteousness of God is the faith of Christ Jesus to all, and upon all believers. There is no difference for all have sinned, and come short of the glory of God. Justified, that is being just in His sight, and validated by grace through the redemption in Christ Jesus, God not only made Christ our righteousness, but made Him our redemption, wisdom, sanctification, and redemption.

There is a cost of faith unto salvation. Those sold under sin, those slaves of sin, and those under the bondage to sin, need to know Jesus as Savior and Lord. Being made a curse under the law, Christ redeemed all from under the curse, and as Redeemer, is made our redemption. Set apart from God, Christ consecrated to make peace through faith in His blood, and declare His righteousness for the remission of sins past, present, and future. Through patience, God being just and the justifier of believers in Christ Jesus, paid the price of salvation through the death of His only begotten Son. Therefore, we conclude that a believer, justified by faith without deeds of the law, perceives all of God, who justifies all by the faith found only in Christ Jesus. (Rom. 3:21-31; 1 Cor. 1:30; Gal. 3:13)

There is yet another element of cost applicable to Salvation: the judgment of God. Why does God appear to be so cruel, while at times merciful, loving, and kind? Is it reasonable to suppose, there may be more, or an easier way to provide salvation for humanity? The way of God, known to the evangelical, rests in the fact of being born again. The Way, the Truth and the Life through Jesus the Christ, is the way of salvation. Yet, in most liberal churches, the term 'born again' is not often used, especially related to salvation.

Some preach the love and tenderness of God as the Mother of creation and even refers to the Mother of Jesus, as being the Mother of God. We often hear the expression, "Oh, my God, or Oh, Dear Mother of God." Some teach God as female. Rightly, among those who attest there are many ways to heaven, and therefore many ways to God. Apparently, the image of a father is too strict and formal for some, whereas the image of a mother is more loving and kind. The simple fact is, God has His way, His method, and to rebuke God is treading on dangerous ground. So, staying in the context of Scripture, what is the way of the righteousness of God.

Suppose God's way of working is similar to man's way of working. In some careers, work is directed by a supervisor, others may be trusted to do the work without supervision. One is tidy and each detail of work rewarding, whereas another jumps in, and does the job without thinking of reward, except that of being paid for the labor. Therefore, we see degrees in methodology, some better than others. What method of work do you suppose God would enlist? Tidy, mediocre, well done, God justified His work as good. Humanity must justify their work, but with different values.

God's way of working reveals His values in the same way as a person working reveals values. An employee works to please the supervisor or boss. God works according to His nature. His works bear a special mark distinguishing them as being of God. His way, and related to His nature, must be the way of righteousness. God cannot do work in a way of unrighteousness. That is the distinguishing point of God's work, His righteousness. It is for this reason, that it poses a problem, not just for God, but humanity. God is love, and therefore His work of salvation must accommodate love. Humanity, dressed in unrighteousness not saved. How then, when the works of humanity call for judgment, God can instill His righteousness. Yes, through the giving of His only begotten Son Jesus, He gave a substitute for humanity.

The judgment of humanity put a heavy load on Father God. What is He, as a loving father, to do? In schools, and public places, Government forbids and hinders the Christian from speaking to strangers that they might believe unto salvation. In so doing, the unbelieving heap upon themselves even greater sins. Thus, the judgment of God must come upon them, even to the uttermost. (John 14:6; 1 Thess. 2:16)

Thank God, that He has provided a way of salvation. Thank God that He is satisfied with His way of provision, for He must declare, "It is good." This book presents the fact of faith, being the way of God. However, where there is no opportunity to declare faith to unbelievers, how much longer will His grace prevail? Even so, come Lord Jesus.

Looking around, what do we see? There is much unrighteousness, and corruption in the marketplace. It would be easy, as God did once before, to rain upon planet earth and swallow up the wicked. In Noah's case, there were only eight out of many souls saved out of the water, the rest drowned.

On the other hand, God could show pity upon each nest of humanity and lift them out of sin, and place them into a safe place, preserving them unto the day of salvation. In each case, we walk away justified, in that they are safe.

Now, you know it is not God's nature to be unfair to those who struggle in maintaining their righteousness. It is not right that some are set free without judgment. Thus, God suffers in a quandary of four possibilities. Obviously, He wants to save, but cannot relax His hold on righteousness. He wants to be merciful, but on the other hand, He must be just. It is His will that He offer salvation, but it must be without compromising His nature of righteousness. God has a plan wherein forgiving is just, yet at the same time, not overlook the cost of original sin.

God has determined a way by which he can satisfy His righteousness, and at same time, keep the law and forgive the sinner. Now, this is Grace, this is unmerited favor, and in Christ, made the righteousness of God. This confirms that in the way of salvation, neither the lost nor the found can complain.

Previously, we saw how a woman sought justice from an unrighteous judge. This Judge had no fear of God or of man. She came and asked, "Avenge me of an adversary." He pondered the request for a while, but afterward thought within himself, "Though I do not fear God, or man, yet this woman troubles me, so to shut her up, he agreed to avenge her. Strange as it may seem, but the Lord said, "Hear what the unjust judge said." He asked, "Shall God not avenge his elect, though they pray day and night, yet He continues to carry them along the way, but I say, He will avenge?"

Then, the Lord grieving for His wayfaring children asked, "When the Son of man comes back to planet earth, shall he find faith"? What question is this? After He has done all in bringing about salvation, grieves over the fact that some may seek yet another way. Remember God's grace, is always governed by His righteousness. (Luke 18:1-8; 1 Cor. 5:21)

Throughout the years, an item and symbol of Christian tradition, is becoming lost on planet earth. You may notice a church is no longer identified by the symbol of the cross. God chose the cross to reveal His righteousness. In view of the law and that of righteousness, the cross is indispensable. The cross reveals sin unto the world, and righteousness unto a Christian. The cost of faith on planet earth is the way of the cross. With its demise, there is no debt, and the sinner found worthy through works of the flesh. Thus, the reading and intent of this book finally realized. There is no other way.

God uses the cross as the method for payment of judgment. Without the cross, there is no receipt showing, "Paid in full." Jesus said, "If any man will come after me, let him deny himself, and take up his cross daily, and follow me." Whosoever follows after the righteousness of God in Christ Jesus will have found eternal Life. Whosoever transgresses the law will bear their punishment. Government knows that, schools know that, and parents know that, but denial shows nothing but self-righteousness. (Luke 9:23; Mat. 16:24)

Salvation is only by means of the cross, upon which Jesus Christ, God absorbed the cost of salvation. The Christian too, must pay the cost through repentance and faith. Jesus, the ultimate sacrifice paid, but we, placed into His death, buried, resurrected, ascended. The efficacy of the cross, paid in full.

Therefore, dear reader, Grace be unto you, and peace, from God our Father, and from the Lord Jesus Christ. I thank God each day on your behalf, for the grace of God given you by Jesus Christ: That in everything enriching you in word and knowledge. The testimony of Christ, being confirmed in you, that you too, come with His gift of faith. Waiting for the coming of our Lord Jesus Christ, He shall confirm unto the end, you as blameless in the day of our Lord Jesus Christ. (1 Cor. 1:4-9)

Further, you have come face to face with this biblical truth. "The Faith of Christ as being crucial unto salvation." In closing, a mother, who in fear her male child would be killed, by faith made for him an ark of bulrushes. Laying her child therein, placed it in a group of cattails by the river. The lad's sister stood afar off to observe the effects of her mother's faith. Soon, the daughter of Pharaoh came down to wash herself at the river; her maidens, walking along the river's bank, saw the ark among the cattails. The daughter, requesting they draw it up from the water, brought the child unto her bosom. The lad's sister watched, fetched her mother, who once again nursed her son, Moses.

The story of Moses, so named because he was saved from the water, began with the faith of his mother. Later, we see how the children of Israel, by the faith of Moses, were all saved out of the water, passed through the Red Sea as by dry land, and as they journeyed, nurtured by the same spiritual food, manna. Though Moses, forbidden from the promise land, his faith is observed today by the Jewish Passover. The Faith of Christ provides for us today, the power to become the children of God, even to them who believe on His Name.

Christian, you are saved from the waters of death, nurtured by the Word of God, so live by the Faith of the Son of God. Do not follow after the way of Cain, because as Pharaoh, you too will drown in the attempt. (Exodus 2:1-10; John 1:1-12; Rom. 6:1-10; 1 Cor. 10:1-10; Eph. 2:1-10; Hebrews 11:24-29)

~

# References

1) The free online encyclopedia, *Wikipedia.*

2) The *King James Version* of the Bible.

3) Universal House of Justice, Haifa, Israel.

   Computers for Christ, San Jose, Ca.

   Jesus is Savior.com.

4) Walter Martins, cults reference Bible.

5) New World Encyclopedia.

6) Instilling Goodness School, Talmage, CA 95481.

7) The Catholic Encyclopedia. dharma.ncf.ca/introduction/truths/karma2.html

8) The Free Dictionary.com.

9) Schaeffer, Francis A. (1976) *How then should we then live?* Fleming H. Revell Company, Old Tappan, New Jersey.

10) *Grace Notes*, Warren Doud, 1705 Aggie Lane, Austin, Texas 78757

11) Copied from MetroLyrics.com Sung BY Johnny Cash – You Tube AducEKFACHY

12) Emotional Bonds Between Leaders and Followers

13) *Charismatic Authority*; by Austin Cline.

14) Tuke G.H. (1882) *Chapters in the history of the insane in the British Isles*, London, Kegan.

15) *The Prayer Labyrinth*, USA Central Territorial Salvation Army Headquarters.

16) *Baha'l* – free on line dictionary.

17) *The Labyrinth Journey: Walking the Path to Fulfillment?* By Carl Teichrib - September 2005. Please visit his website at www.forcingchange.org

18) The Pew Form Organization. http://www.pewforum.org

19)   The Labyrinth Company – USC.salvationarmy.org
      /.../04733F30A97716F5862575E4006843B7?

20)   Charles R. Solomon, *Ins and Outs of Rejection*, copyright
      1991.

21)   George Somerville, drgeo@telus.net  Web page–
      www.weegeordie.ca

22)   More.ca *The evolution of the high divorce rate* Deborah
      Moskovitch

23)   Statistics Canada to stop tracking marriage and divorce
      rates – Tavia Grant. The Globe and Mail

24)   Dana Hinders Web page    http://divorce.lovetoknow.com/
      Divorce_Statistics

25)   Joshua Collins, *The Knowledge of Good and Evil*,  2008
      GlobalEdAdvance Press

26)   *The Word-Faith Movement* - By Gary E. Gilley.

27)   Ted Brooks, *The Flaky Preacher* (1999) Guardian Books,
      Ontario, Canada

28)   Watchman Nee, *The Glory of His Life.*

29)   *Living Systems*, by James G. Miller.

30)   Character First Web Page - www.characterfirst.com

31)   Eddie Snipes - Exchanged Life Outreach.

32)   Mathew Henry's Commentary.

33)   *The Christian Approach to Philosophy* – W. Young.

34)   *Abortion Rates*,  Liz Olson - Infoplease.com

35)   *Why Churches Die*  Hollis L Green, 2008,
      GlobalEdAdvance Press.

36)   Home Evangel Book Shop, Toronto, Ontario.

37)   *New Dictionary of Thoughts*, Standard Book Co.

38)   Let us Reason Ministries - http://www.letusreason.org

39)   David J. Stewart, www.Jesus is Savior.com.

40)   Mountainview – Tony Warren – Faith of Christ.
      www.mountainretreatorg.net/bible/faithof.html

www.ingramcontent.com/pod-product-compliance
Lightning Source LLC
Chambersburg PA
CBHW052112090426
42741CB00009B/1780